A H

LISDOONVARNA

AND

ITS VICINITY.

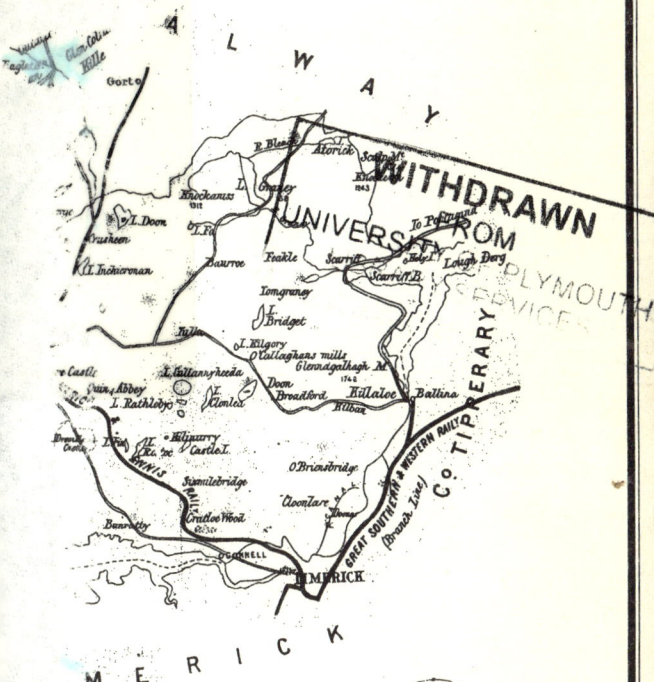

ROUTE MAP OF
LISDOONVARNA
Cº CLARE.

A HAND BOOK

TO

LISDOONVARNA

AND

ITS VICINITY.

WITH MAP AND WOODCUTS.

GIVING A DETAILED ACCOUNT OF ITS
CURATIVE WATERS, AND TOURS TO
THE PRINCIPAL PLACES OF INTEREST
IN THE COUNTY CLARE.

P. D.

CLASP PRESS

CLASP PRESS,
Clare County Library Headquarters,
Mill Road, Ennis, Co. Clare.

This edition © CLASP PRESS, 1998.
First edition Hodges, Foster & Co.,
Dublin, 1876.

ISBN 1 900545 06 3

Design & layout by Jackie Dermody.

Typed by CLASP personnel.

Cover design by Anthony Edwards.
Cover layout by Siobhán McCooey.
Cover photograph, Lawrence Collection,
courtesy National Library of Ireland.

Printed by ColourBooks, Dublin.

This edition is limited to 1000 copies.

CONTENTS

———————◆———————

CHAIRMAN'S INTRODUCTION

———◆———

Clare Local Studies Project (CLASP) was set up as an independent organisation by members of Clare Library Staff to develop awareness and increase access to sources for local studies in County Clare. Since May 1995 its formal partnership with FÁS and its informal links with Clare County Council have been an outstanding success. This present publication by CLASP PRESS follows the previous titles *County Clare: A History and Topography, Poverty Before the Famine, County Clare 1835, Two Months at Kilkee, Kilrush Union Minute Books 1849* and *Sable Wings over the Land*.

This publication is enhanced by the addition of a delightful introduction by author and poet, Cyril Ó Céirín. Cyril's roots are firmly planted in Lisdoonvarna with a family connection stretching back over two centuries. All those visitors who have fond memories of time spent in Lisdoonvarna will enjoy a trip down memory lane and will gain a greater insight into the origins and development of Lisdoonvarna and its environs.

The talents and hard work of the FÁS trainees has resulted in making this long out of print guide available once again. I would particularly like to congratulate Jackie Dermody in her design and lay-out. It is obvious that Jackie has benefited greatly from her time with CLASP.

Finally, I would like to thank our friends in FÁS for the constant help and encouragement.

Noel Crowley

ACKNOWLEDGEMENTS

———◆———

The trainees on the CLASP team began working on this publication in the autumn of 1997. The early stages of the publication involved the typing of the original text onto computers followed by the inevitable task of proof-reading.

Many trainees were involved in the production of this publication and I would like to take this opportunity to recognise their commitment to the project, particularly, Joyce Cronin, Lorna Downes, Michelle Moroney, Katie Kearney, Siobhán Kenny, Tracey Hayes, Maria Meaney and Linda Burke. I would also like to give special thanks to our Senior Trainee, Sharon Considine-Meaney, who was with this project from the beginning.

This publication would not have been possible without the commitment and dedication of Noel Crowley, County Librarian and Anthony Edwards, Executive Librarian. I would like to thank them for their continued enthusiasm and support of the project. I would also like to thank Maureen Comber, Local Studies Librarian and Ted Finn, Executive Librarian for their final proof-reading of the text and their valuable suggestions. Finally, I would like to thank Jacqueline Dermody, my predecessor, who initially supervised this publication. I would like to acknowledge the support and assistance that we have received from FÁS, especially Donal Griffin, External Training Manager.

Martina Crowley-Hayes
Project Supervisor.

INTRODUCTION

———◆———

The beneficial effects of the mineral waters near Lisdoonvarna, County Clare, were first noted at some time before the middle of the eighteenth century. (I say 'near Lisdoonvarna' advisedly as the nearest known well in those days, the Rathbawn Spring, is a good Irish mile and a half from the Lisdoonvarna castle site after which the later spa complex was to be named.) The first recorded analysis of the water was made as early as 1751. A half century later, Hely Dutton in his *Statistical Survey of Clare* wrote that the Spa had been long celebrated, adding caustically that visitors, who could not avail of the several landlords' 'big houses' in the area, had to do with 'damp, dirty lodgings in cabins', most likely in the small *baile* at Rooska to the west of Rathbawn House. In 1803, the traveller, Woods, recorded that the spa was 'much frequented'. Yet, despite the fact that by 1837 a few cottages had been built expressly for visitors (Pierce Creagh, the landlord on whose property at Rathbawn the then principal well was, being interested in the potential of the resource), the Ordnance Survey map of 1840 shows only three houses in the area which was to contain the main part of Lisdoonvarna Spa Town. Incidentally, the well at Gowlaun, now known far and wide as the Sulphur Well and the main attraction for a hundred and thirty years, is marked but there is no indication at all of its being a spa.

In the intervening century and a half, Lisdoonvarna has become one of the more famous (perhaps even the most remarkable) of resorts in Ireland, a phenomenon celebrated in song (one reached the top of the charts), in story, in international magazines and in TV programmes. Its mushroom growth and subsequent development in the latter part of the nineteenth century and the first decades of this one may well seem surprising in the light of the general historical context of the period. A hotel of sorts had indeed been built before the Great Famine. (Enlarged later and known since as the Royal Spa, it is happily still in operation.) A sub-post office and, surprisingly, another 'hotel' had been built during that famine, but Griffith's Valuations some handful of years later shows only sixteen houses in that area which was to become Lisdoonvarna. The resort found its feet quite rapidly after the devastation. In 1852, the Gowlaun or Sulphur Spring having being recently discovered, some locals began work on the surrounding area, aided by a grant received through the good offices of their landlord, Capt. William Stacpoole. By 1859, there were some sixty houses and, the spa's reputation having 'increased as a most desirable resort for the Invalid and Tourist', the first church was built: a Church of Ireland Chapel of Ease 'adequate to the numbers (of visitors)'. Up to this, the bulk of 'Invalids and Tourists' had been drawn from the Protestant gentry, professionals and 'strong farmers', but the new, rising class of Roman Catholic big farmers was also following the fashion of 'taking the waters' in ever-increasing numbers. (An old resident of 'The Spa', whose grandfather had been evicted at this time, once remarked to me sourly that they all badly needed the cleansing effects of the sulphur after 'long winters spent eating too much salt beef and drinking too much bad whiskey'.) The improved status of many Roman Catholics in this period is evidenced by the fact that a Catholic Chapel of Ease was built ten years later (the parish church remaining for many more years at Toomaghera, two and a half miles distant). The present-day Roadside Tavern is recorded in this era, but not as a tavern; ideally situated opposite the Rathbawn Spring, it was most likely a lodging house or shop. It is hard to credit, but up to this time turf was still being cut in what was to become The Square and focal point of the town. Nevertheless, it could be said that at least Lisdoonvarna was now on the map

It was certainly in the news. Captain Stacpoole, landlord of the Gowlaun area, had attempted to take over the sulphur spring for his own commercial benefit, ignoring the fact that a public right of way existed, probably from the time a water-mill had been in operation on the site. Stacpoole built two small houses, installed a pump and blocked the right of way with walls and gates. (It is not unlikely that he was abetted in the enterprise by his kinsman, Dr. Westropp, who was to be one of the co-authors of this *Handbook to Lisdoonvarna*). These were Fenian times and the right of public access was asserted by dynamite. A later course case upheld this right.

In 1869, the *Clare Journal*, announcing 'contemplated improvements' on Captain Creagh's property in Rathbawn, concluded that 'every inducement will be held out to purchasers to invest their money and, from the increasing popularity of the spas, it seems not improbable that a great social revolution is about to be wrought in this celebrated district.' In 1870, one thousand five hundred people visited the Spas. In the same year, on a site close to the Gowlaun Spring, then the principal well, a first-class hotel, The Eagle, later to become the famous Thomond, was opened. (This hotel, after several decades in ruin, was reopened as the King Thomond some few years ago.) In 1872, a Limerick group laid the foundations of another large hotel, The Queen's, which is the present-day Hydro. This was quickly followed by the Atlantic View Hotel, now the Stella Maris Nursing Home, and the Imperial Hotel, which still maintains its commanding position on the Sulphur Hill. The great majority of other buildings in the village were lodging houses. The Midland Great Western Railway was advertising among its Summer Excursions one which they proclaimed was 'the cheapest, shortest and most enjoyable route to the Celebrated Spas of Lisdoonvarna'. The Galway Steamboat Company was running its steamer, 'City of the Tribes', from Galway to Ballyvaughan daily for 'the season'. In 1878, five thousand visitors came to 'The Spa'.

*   *   *   *

It was during this booming period, in 1876, that this book, *A Handbook to Lisdoonvarna and its Vicinity*, appeared. It has long been held that its main author, who identified himself only as 'P. D.', was the Rev. Canon Philip Dwyer, Church of Ireland vicar *cum* rector of the important parish of Drumcliffe, Ennis, from 1864 to 1883. (Incidentally, when a long-time resident of Lisdoonvarna loaned me her copy of the *Handbook* quite a few years ago, she whispered conspiratorially, as if the secret contained some strange significance, that the author was indeed Canon Dwyer.) However reluctant 'P. D.' was to give his full name, he frankly acknowledged that the 'very important chapter' on the Spas of Lisdoonvarna, which gave a thorough analysis of the three major wells of the time, was based on extracts from a report made by a Mr. Plunkett of the Royal College of Science and by a Mr. Launcelot Studdert, LL. D., who prepared and supplemented it for the *Handbook*. 'P. D.' was also eager to acknowledge that the chapter on the Medicinal Properties and Effects of the Spas of Lisdoonvarna was the work of Dr. Westrop (*sic*) of Lisdoonvarna. This Dr. William Henry Stacpoole Westropp was closely related to the great antiquarian T. J. Westropp and also, most importantly, to the Captain Stacpoole on whose property was the Gowlaun Spring. Dr. Westropp supervised the building of the first bathhouse here, at the 'Sulphur Wells', and, in the year before the *Handbook* was published, had built the beautiful gothic-style Maiville House directly overlooking the Wells. Not unnaturally, he and Captain Stacpoole were intent on exploiting the commercial potential of their spa - an ambition not necessarily incompatible with 'P.D.'s earnest assertion in the *Handbook* that the writers were publishing it from a duty 'to alleviate human suffering and to promote innocent recreation.' If the main author was indeed Canon Dwyer, it is not unlikely that he was coy about giving his full title as it might be thought inappropriate that a clergyman of his status would be so closely associated with commerce.

There has been some recent speculation that Dwyer was not 'P. D.' at all, the name of Pender Downes, a notable journalist with the *Clare Journal* at the time, being suggested instead. However, internal evidence might be judged to support the claim of the earlier tradition. The *Handbook*, for instance, contains a full-page advertisement appealing to 'the Christian liberality of the members of the Church of Ireland, of her friends, and of the sojourners of Lisdoonvarna' for contributions towards the building of a new church, the old one being too small to contain the recent increase in holiday-makers; Canon Dwyer is listed as a member of the church building committee, as also are Captain Stacpoole and two members of the Studdert family. The *Handbook* also contains asides more fitting, perhaps, to a clergyman than to a journalist (though it has to be admitted that Victorian journalists could be as sanctimonious as any of the former). More significant are 'P.D.'s enthusiastic and knowledgeable references to early Christian sites which are entirely compatible with the material and sentiments contained in a major historical work published three years later, *The Diocese of Killaloe from the Reformation to the close of the Eighteenth Century*, and written by the Revd. Canon Philip Dwyer in question.

The reason behind my Lisdoonvarna informant's air of secrecy may well have arisen from one of Dwyer's aims as a historian, that of pressing the claims of the Church of Ireland to be the religion proper to the Irish people, who, in his opinion, had abandoned the religion of the Early Christian period for Roman Catholicism after the Norman invasions. His *Diocese of Killaloe* offended Catholics for, as one reviewer diplomatically put it, he had 'gone somewhat out of his way in our humble judgement to spoil his work with the impress of occasional sectarianism.' The *Handbook*, obviously aimed at the wealthy Protestant classes (though it contains no anti-Catholic sentiments) probably was looked upon with suspicion by Roman Catholics after the hullabaloo over his later book had arisen. In 1883, Canon Dwyer unexpectedly surrendered his incumbency and went as a missionary to British Columbia. He returned to die in Somerset, England. Born at Uskane, County Tipperary, Canon Dwyer was a scion of the once-powerful Gaelic and Roman Catholic family, the Uí Dhuíbhir, whose principal seat was at Kilmanagh, County Tipperary.

Of one thing there is no doubt: the *Handbook* is not only a highly informative but an enjoyable and sometimes charming book, with nuggets of pure gold for the social historian and ordinary reader alike. Unquestionably, the author knew the area and its people from Liscannor to Oughtmama and Blackhead to Killinaboy. He was also well-acquainted with - and not at all ashamed of - the history of Gaelic Ireland and the Early Christian Church here.

*   *   *   *

After 1876, Lisdoonvarna developed even more rapidly and, with the coming of the West Clare Railway to Ennistymon in 1887, probably outstripped the most sanguine expectations of 'P.D.', Westropp and Stacpoole. There was to be one major difference, however: by 1895, when twenty thousand visitors came to 'The Spa', the Stacpoole property was in chancery and a Local Improvements Committee (in practice a form of co-operative) had a seven-year lease on the Sulphur Wells and Grounds. They built a pump house and new baths and successfully resisted - in court and by public protest and forcible action - a sustained attempt by the Church of Ireland Representative Body, in whom the Stacpoole property was vested, and two local businessmen to take the Wells from the 'people of Lisdoonvarna'. In 1906, the Eagle Hotel was re-opened as the Thomond and no less a personage than Lord Aberdeen, Lord Lieutenant of Ireland, did the honours; this was probably the greatest night in the history of the Spa and gave the resort a further enormous boost. By this time, of course, there were more hotels to bear witness to the general prosperity: The Glenbourne, Keanes, Garrahies, Lynchs, the Ravine and the Inisfail, and several fine lodging houses such as Sheedy's Spa

View House and Kerin's Atlantic View House whose owners felt not the least bit uncomfortable when their 'visitors' referred to them as 'hotels'.

In 1915, the long-standing legal problems being finally resolved, the Improvements Association was incorporated under the Scheme for the Regulation and Management of the Lisdoonvarna and Rooska Spa Wells Trust. The halcyon days continued, despite the World War, the War of Independence and the Civil War. Not so, however, during the Economic War, when farmers and farming industries suffered most. Then the Second World War put a brake on recovery. In 1943, a new company, the Lisdoonvarna Improvements Association, was established 'to undertake without remuneration' the management of the property of the Spa Wells Trust. Many residents of the town will still recall the general excitement and optimism at the war's end as they prepared to bring back 'the old days'. It was not to be: the general depression and emigration continued for more than a decade and, with the rising of the economic tide of the sixties, modern transport and new fashions were already making the traditional holiday a thing of the past. The visitor industry in Lisdoonvarna, now carried only by its own momentum, continued to wind down and the Wells lumbered on, but from crisis to crisis.

*   *   *   *

In 1976, the High Court accepted a new scheme for the regulation and management of the Spa Wells Trust and a new company (limited by guarantee),

Lisdoonvarna Fáilte, was formed. By this time, the wells were of far less importance as a visitor attraction than the image summed up in the slogan 'Lisdoonvarna for the Crack!' or the promotion of events such as Rock concerts, the much longer-lived Matchmaking Festivals and the World Barbecue Championships. Tied up by legalities, financial constraints and lack of investment among other things, Lisdoonvarna Fáilte, who at least kept the Wells open and its head (barely) above water for more than two decades, attempted unsuccessfully to turn the complex over to an outside interest, but after five years of negotiations the potential investment fell through. The most recent board of directors find themselves with an unenviable dilemma: lobby for tax designation status for Lisdoonvarna and put faith in private investment, a course with obvious dangers as well as immediate benefits for both the Wells and the town; or seek both adequate financial backing and a suitable managerial entity or lessee, a policy which, however desirable, seems to have little chance of success. In either case, somehow the spas have to be kept open.

The Wells, through the Trust, belongs to the 'people of Lisdoonvarna' - whatever interpretation a High Court might put on that appellation today. For over a century and a half, the 'people of Lisdoonvarna', through a mixture of co-operation, hard work, enterprise, independence and sometimes sheer doggedness, have developed and kept their spas open, even when under threat from landlords, speculators and depressions; it is to be hoped that the present generation will not let them go by default.

*   *   *   *

In writing this introduction, I am indebted to the generous (and cheerful) assistance of Maureen Comber, Local Studies Librarian, and of Anthony Edwards, Executive Librarian, both of Clare County Library. For information on Canon Dwyer, I have gratefully drawn on the researches of Ignatius Murphy in his *Diocese of Killaloe 1850 - 1904* (Four Courts Press, 1995) and of Tim Kelly in his *Ennis in the Nineteenth Century* (M.A. Thesis, 1971). I would also like to pay tribute to Sr. de Lourdes Fahy's ground-breaking lecture *Origin and Growth of Lisdoonvarna 1750 - 1900* (Scoil Merriman, 1986).

Cyril Ó Céirín

Lios Dúin Bhearna, 1998.

PREFACE

————◆————

IMPRESSED with the persuasion that those who had it in their power to communicate information calculated to alleviate human suffering and to promote innocent recreation were bound to use that power, the writers undertook the task of preparing and publishing the following little book.

The very important chapter, viz., No. III., bearing, at its close, the initials "L.S." is the substance of a paper on the Spas of Lisdoonvarna lately read by Launcelot Studdert, Esq., LL.D., before the Royal Irish Academy, and now further supplemented to exhibit of the analytic results arrived at by him as to Lisdoonvarna Spas, as compared with those recorded of other Spas in England, Ireland, Scotland and the Continent of Europe.

The next chapter, No. IV., gives a very careful statement of the medicinal effects resulting from the use of the Lisdoonvarna waters. It is written by a medical man who has made this subject a special study, and who, living on the spot, has gathered a large experience of results to be obtained and of requirements to be attended to. This chapter, signed "S.W." is the valued contribution of Dr. Westrop, of Lisdoonvarna.

The other chapters are but the framework in which the learning and skill of the Analyst and Doctor are set. They bear the initials

"P. D."

ENNIS, *June 1st, 1876.*

CHAPTER I.

———◆———

AMONG the many travellers who seek Lisdoonvarna's far-famed Spas, whether for sake of health or recreation, some may be fairly presumed to have more or less time at their disposal, and a desire to become acquainted with whatever may prove interesting or instructive, whether occurring along the way or in the adjacent regions of the wild West.

Accordingly our friend, as we may be allowed so to speak on a slight acquaintance, may be supposed to have reached the confines of the County Clare by some of the trains discharging from the eastern or south-eastern parts of Ireland.

Such we receive with all due honour at Limerick, or at Killaloe "down by the Shannon shore."

KILLALOE.

Approaching the terminus the eye is caught by a singularly brilliant little Island of verdant pasture, Friars Island is its name, and on it stands, though somewhat dilapidated, an Oratory attributed to Mollua. The authorities declare that the name of the Diocese of Killaloe comes from Killomollua.

There stands still the old structure insignificant in dimensions and unpretentious as to ornament. Its stone-pointed roof is down; but the marks fitted for an insertion of this kind of covering remain.

1

The late Mr. Brash a careful and accurate architect and observer, has given the exact dimensions and a good sketch in his valuable work on the ecclesiastical architecture of Ireland.

If we cross the bridge, from which are very fine views, we find another very fine Oratory of the pointed and stone roofed class in a state of wondrous good preservation, having been repaired some twenty-four years ago by the pious and patriotic care of the Rev. William Edwards, A.M., now Rector of Lisburn. The door ways are comparatively modern, being a decorative reparation inserted by order of Brian Borhoime, the great King of Ireland.

How striking are the proofs which these two quaint structures give of the devotion and judgement of the early standard bearers of the cross.

These hermits, Lua and Flannan, settle on either side of the ford, that they might tell the news they had to tell as best they could, to the wayfarers passing and repassing between eastern and western Thomond on errands of war or pleasure; rather indeed chiefly bent on cattle-plundering, which had a sweet blended relish of both. The Cathedral stands adjacent to St. Flannan's Oratory. It is a solid simple structure, bearing traces of an earlier edifice preceding, not only in the Romanesque doorway inserted in the south-western wall of the nave, but also in other details duly recorded in the Chapter Book. The demesne of Clarisford or Claresford, the Bishop's seat, is beautifully situated. The house was almost rebuilt by Bishop Fowler in the last century.

The pleasure grounds are ornate and well kept, and an old ornamental cross removed from Kilfenora crowns a rich vista of foliage, with its stately proportions.

LOUGH DERG.

And now if our friend is pleased with this first impression of the county in which he proposes to sojourn, we would suggest an evening drive, such as is not often to be had. Our road runs by Ballyvalley, the seat of Robert Parker, Esq., and ere long we reach a broad grassy mound or terrace opening towards the lake on the right. Here tradition has placed the kingly halls of the great Brian Borhoime, fit site for a royal residence is this Kincora, *"the head of the weir."* As we ascend the height of Tinnerana, a view opens at the windy gap, north, south, east, and west, over which cold indeed must be at the heart of him who would not love to linger. Here is "the mighty Shenan spreading like an inland sea." There to the left the hills of Broadford rear their heads and slopes clothed in the rich tints of heath and gorse. On the right the lawns and fields and groves of Derry, nestle snugly under the wild confused refuse heaps of the great slate quarries. And now turning back towards Limerick, you have the Shannon (Father of Waters) glittering with golden sheen in the glowing sun of the evening as he pursues his course towards his destination in the west.

Tomgraney is soon reached, and if our friend has any antiquarian taste, he will not scorn that old church which Petrie and others before and since have visited and scanned, and measured, and pictured, and speculated upon, and intensely admired, and of course fiercely fought about. The grand old building was even dragged into the controversy about the age of the earliest stone buildings in Ireland. There is the Cyclopean western wall and the doorway with sloping jambs, all in good preservation - meet emblem the structure of an honest man's work. On the out-side, rough perhaps to look at, but solid, well designed and long to live for good.

And now we have reached Scariff, so called from the broken, rough torrent which flows through it from the hills. Who has not heard of its lazar-house in the sad times of the famine from 1847, and of its poor rates that eat up the rent, and of its paupers, and how many grave-yards grew fat with their miserable mortality?

Moynoe brings us nearer to that gem of villages Mountshannon-Daly, in Co. Galway. Here a colony of Northern weavers settled about one hundred years ago, and wrought away happily until Arkwright's power-looms beggared and scattered them. And now ferried across a narrow strait of the Great Lough Derg, which is twenty miles long, and thirteen at its greatest breadth, we stand upon

Here is to be traced, though not without an effort, the original Oratory which, scanty as it was, sufficed for the simple life of the first adventurous hermit. Here, too, stand more or less of the other churches and buildings, and, over all, the lofty round tower - a belfry it was, say some - the symbol of a strange extinct worship say others - and a Cuthite institution say a few more. Prehistoric conjectures certainly have this pleasant advantage, that you may set up any theories you please, but then, on the other hand, any one else with equal fearlessness of assertion, may set up other theories to the contrary. But there stand the buildings in which St. Camin wrote out a copy of the Psalms of David, and collated them with the Hebrew text. The buildings survive the wars of the Gaedil and Gaelgi. There, too, are the monumental slabs inserted in the walls, commemorating to a forgetful futurity the proud Mac O' Briens of Arra; there, too, until recent times were held Patterns and Rounds, with an amount of reckless dissipation closing the religious proceeding, happily now discontinued.

THE SHANNON TROUT.

But what about the fishing, one will say? Is there any, and where? Fishing indeed there is. When the May-fly, having split up and struggled out of his *pupa*, which had sheltered him all winter through upon the marly bottom of the lake, now rises to the surface between 11 a.m. and 3 p.m. on some life-stirring day in May, and, before he has well-nigh aired his saffron body on a flake of foam, or expanded his tissued wings, is rushed at by the "old ones," usually of from 3 lbs. to 10 lbs., which now grow ravenous and reckless in snapping at the luscious morsel, or any thing at all like it. Let not thy grave wisdom censure, oh, friend, let not even thy legal horsehair stand virtuously on end, if legal thou art. Remember that the poor, over-driven worker may once and again take a day or two with rod in hand amid these fishing grounds of the fortunate, and return to work a giant refreshed. Days like these have induced the renowned Jonathan Henn, leader of the Irish Bar, to fling back heavy briefs, and heavier fees to the importunate attorney. Gentle Walton never knew of the like, no nor the erudite author of Salmonia, &c.

The Gilleroo trout is not found in this immediate shore. To reach him you must fetch north to Coös Bay. His gizzard may be a fine speculation to exercise the naturalists, his gymnastics are enough for the sportsman.

But now we must needs tear ourselves away from this scene of enchantment. Friend, take thy last look of that fair isle, dotted over with fattening bullocks and snowy sheep, and of church and refectory, and those ivy-clad walls, and that lofty tower, all standing out so full and clear, as they break the long lines of Lough Derg's surface and are caught in the mellowing tints of the background formed by Youghal-arra and Duharrow hills on the Tipperary shore. We must go and turn from the fading traces of a day that is past to contemplate the practical utilities and growing beauties of modern improvement.

Mr. Henry Coutler, in his "West of Ireland," gives a valuable detailed statement of the improvements executed, during a long and useful life, by Philip Reade, Esq., J.P., upon a wild and heathery mountain-side, which now presents every feature of high and judicious land-improvement, and returns ample profits too, among which, not the least prized by this exemplary country gentleman and his many friends, is the honourable and patriotic sense of his life of well-doing.

Other Co. Clare gentlemen have been alike most praiseworthy improvers in East Clare, among whom may stand the late James Moloney, Esq., J.P., D.L., of Kiltanon, Tulla.

CASTLE CONNELL.

The traveller or tourist who passes from Killaloe to Limerick too often loses a rare jem of river beauty. And as our friend may have visited with us a broad lake of the Shannon, so we would now pass along side of the tumbling roaring stream which forces his way in mad foaming eddies from Castle Connell over the Salmon Leap of Doonas and onward to Limerick with sobering speed. For us to attempt a verbal description of these scenes would be the extreme of presumption. Wilfully to pass by unvisited this "roar of waters" amid verdure and variety at once endless and enchanting, would be simple infatuation. Let the carriage drive to Castle Connell first, and be sent round by O'Brien's Bridge through Clonlara and wait at the river's brink. Meanwhile we are ferried in cots across to the Clare side, and enjoy such a walk as none can forget who has capacity for treasuring up the sublime and beautiful, and enriching himself withal.

"The falls of Doonas and Hermitage are some of the finest in the united kingdom. Here the whole Shannon is impelled with tremendous force and deafening noise, over a succession of craggy limestone rocks, down a descent of fifty-five and a half feet in about half a mile, and this spot is perhaps unequalled in its situation and water power for hill sites, and almost unrivalled in its picturesque beauties. Here the sublime and beautiful are united, and the lovers of nature may revel in scenery congenial to their various tastes; here are assembled the foaming cascade, the rushing torrent, the boiling flood, the craggy rock, the gently swelling lawn, the frowning cliff, the retiring vale, the wooded hill, the noble mansion, and the peaceful cottage embosomed in woods. Here is the spot for those who love to study or enjoy nature, where the poet, the philosopher, the sentimentalist, the engineer, and the sportsman may alike find food for the body and mind. - *Fitzgerald and McGregor's "Limerick."*

Of Limerick one must say but little, yet let not the grand old Cathedral of St. Mary's be turned away from even by the slave of time. It is now opened out to the river by the removal of an unsightly range of decayed houses and is about to undergo extensive repairs under the able direction of Dean Bunbury. This fine old Cathedral will deeply interest from many precious traces of the past so happily connected with the present by judicious touches of scientific reparation. The Treaty Stone is also near at hand on the Clare side.

THE LOWER SHANNON.

Once embarked on the Shannon you cannot easily leave until you trace its noble and varied progress to the end. Indeed this river seems from an early period to have fascinated the stranger and the Saxon, and was counted worthy of most exact and careful description, even so far back as in the days of the Tudors.

Starting from Limerick Quay, if possible at an early hour, we are sped in our steamer past the leafy bowers of Tervoe, and the hill of Carrig-O'Gonnell so often an object of contention in the warlike days of Henry VIII. and of Queen Bess. Lord Limerick has now crowned its crest with a castle of imposing style and dimensions.

BUNRATTY.

Bunratty Castle nestles amid rich woods at the mouth of the Raite. The first castle was built by

Robert De Mucegros in 1275, and was obviously held in high importance as a vantage-point against the Irish rebels. Soon it passed into the hands of De Clare. In the year 1646, it was given up to the Parliamentarian fleet. It is now used as a Police Barrack. The walls are very perfect. Near hand is a little old church in ruins and a grass field of wondrous fattening power.

THE FERGUS

Soon opens with its rich and clustering islands, once the resort of great herds of deer, and still not without interest from valuable remains of ecclesiastical antiquity.

The Shannon fed with confluents from Kerry and Clare - the Raite, Faile, Gaile, Maigue, and Cashan, now spreads into a noble volume of waters. But Foynes, like many another advantage of Ireland, is little availed of. Nothing beyond a man-of-war, and occasional timber or pork-laden vessel from Canada, or the States, or else a grain vessel from the Black Sea, usually reposes on its deep capacious bosom.

How different the aspect of the river leading to Liverpool. Let it be remembered that those who may not admire river navigation at the expense of early rising, can start by train from Limerick, and catch the steamer at Foynes. "The best anchorage for large ships off this Island, is S.E. by E. from Chiracon House, and S.S.E. from a small island in 6 to 12 fathoms. The ground good, Spring tides rise 16 feet, and neap tides 8." Piloting Directions.

Is a charming eminence well wooded and carefully kept by Colonel White, the Lieutenant of the County Clare.

THE SOUTHERN ROUTE TO LISDOONVARNA.

Having received at Limerick the visitors approaching Lisdoonvarna, by the Great Eastern Route, we now at Tarbert Roads have the pleasure of welcoming those who are coming by the Southern Route. Among these may be found not a few foreigners, and our American cousins too, who land at Cork, visit Glengariff, do Killarney, take train for Tralee, and car for Tarbert. To these and our other friends we point out the Churchyard of Killymer over on the north shore in which a monument has been erected by R. W. C. Reeves, Esq. to the Colleen Bawn or Ellen Hanly. Her body was thrown in at Moyne Point. A spliced rope attached to it and remarkable for a blue thread, also a peculiarity in the formation of the teeth in her upper jaw serving with other evidence to identify the body and fix guilt on the murderers. They were both executed in Limerick, the principal in 1819, and the accomplice in 1820, the latter alone confessing the crime.

SCATTERY ISLAND.

How bravely stands out the Island of Scattery before us! Its noble round tower is a landmark to the homebound.

The Saint Senanus had hard work, if we accept tradition, in the double battle he must fight, first against the serpent or *pîach*, and then against the Lady who would land near his lonely home, of which latter Tom Moore has so sweetly sung. His bell is in the Royal Irish Academy. His name is borne by many of the locals.

Here also for a while sojourned another celebrity, though in a different line and of modern times. *Charles Lever, M. D.* was stationed at Kilrush by order of the Central Board of Health during the

12

Cholera outbreak in 1832. And here it was that after severe scientific labours, day after day, to save life and alleviate suffering, he used to meet now and then on an evening some of the local wits and savants, one of whom was Mr. Jackson well known by the *alias* of Terry O'Driscoll. These formed a kind of social board of health. Many a pleasant night they passed with Lever, admiring him more and more, and much curious folk-lore they disclosed and discussed. All this took place at "The Hotel." Here turned up the story of "The Thing you Know at the Door for Miss Kitty," arising out of a simple incident in the difficulty of family locomotion in a donkey cart. Here too the fiction of Father Malachy was spun out (by the way Brennan was his manservant's name, Duggan his own), and here was spread that never to be forgotten banquet in which punch, piety, and pleasantry, reigned supreme, until _____. The original of this was a facetious description of the wedding of a farmer's daughter in Kilraghtis Parish near Ennis.

N'importe - the genius of Lever, whose father by the way was an architect, built up everything in the right time and place, and gave to each person the proper colour and air in his brilliant tableaux vivants of Irish life.

KILKEE.

Passing to Kilkee we find admirable accommodation, and may take an evening stroll in highly ozonized and invigorating air along the cliffs which are not easily described or forgotten. The following account of this much admired coast scenery is submitted. It is taken from the pen of a lady who was so deeply impressed by the attractive influences of this watering place that she published, "Two Months at Kilkee."

"In following the numerous and ever-varying bays, heads, and stupendous island rocks, whose untiring scenery would far exceed my ability or space to describe. I must therefore leave to my readers the agreeable employment of examining for themselves amongst the ruins of a coast which has for thousands of winters been assailed by the overwhelming force of the mountain billow of ocean, winged on by the westerly tempest.

"Ruins of nature may be expected after centuries of such assaults. In some places they stand far out from the cliffs as Bishop and Bird Islands, which are immense masses 150 feet high.

"No doubt exists that these islands were once united to the mainland."

In Mr. Wakeman's valuable Handbook of Irish Antiquities, attention is directed to a fine and hitherto unnoticed example on Bishop's Island near Kilkee, of the Bee-hive house. It measures in circumference 115 feet, and is otherwise very remarkable. An Oratory attributed to St. Senan is also adjacent. This wild spot is called by the Irish "the Island of the hungry or starving Bishop." Access is only to be gained by a skilful climber in calm weather.

A quarter of a mile from the amphitheatre is the Puffing Rock from which in certain states of wind and tide, the water is spouted up with a booming sound and descends as mist glittering when the sun shines in a rainbow arch.

A glance across "Lookout Bay" beneath the cliffs presents a picture of the ravages of ocean seldom equalled.

In the furthest angle of this bay is situated a celebrated cavern in which there is a beautiful variety of rich metallic tinges and an astonishing echo.

Intrinsic Bay is an awful recess which gets the name from a vessel fearfully shipwrecked some forty years ago. She dragged her anchors and came near the rocks; a lady emerged from the cabin, and looking round, sank on her knees in an attitude of prayer. The vessel was soon shattered in ten thousand pieces. Just as the Intrinsic went down a seagull descended and picked up out of the water what had proved to be a lady's glove, dropping it inland.

THE PROMONTORY.

The natural bridges of Ross and the promontory of Loops-Head, considered by some the most Westerly projection of Ireland are wild and grand in a high degree, and especially so when a series of gales has rolled in the great breakers. These lashed into rage ungovernable have oft upheaved the solid cliff itself, and piled detached masses of shattered stone in a wild confusion. Strange and weird-like are the local tales of Carrigaholt Castle - How the surprised lover faced his steed at the battlements and desperately escaped, also how Lord Clare's wild yellow Dragoons still ride at night upon the yeasty waves. This region also, like certain parts of Devon, is said to have been somewhat addicted to smuggling in the last century. But we must leave Kilkee and its pleasant strand, and those sheer rocks at the Duggerna from which so many plunge for a morning swim. This place is largely frequented in Summer, and a Railway to Kilrush was in contemplation but has proved a failure somehow or other. This is to be regretted. And being now well on the road northward along the coast-line we are approaching Annageiragh Cascade. Look down at that lake fenced from the sea by a long mound of rounded beech stones.

LOUGH DONALD AND TROMEROE.

This is Lough Donald where oft the white and brown trout and an occasional salmon have rewarded the skill of the angler. Onwards towards the sea is a tall lonely pile; this is Tromeroe. A tragic tale attaches interest to this place. Mr. Hardiman relates it in full detail in his edition of O'Flaherty's West Connaught. Next to the castle is a large modern building used for a coastguard station; yonder to the east (by the way everything in these regions is distinguished as east and west, even to a turnip in a cow's throat or the saddle on a horse's back) there in the hollow of the hill lies Doolic Lake to which St. Senanus banished the serpent from Scattery; all which with many other wonders of the west were described in an Irish romance written in the last century by Mr. Michael Comyn, who lived in Kilcornan.

THE OGHAM INSCRIPTION ON MOUNT CALLAN.

This gentleman, who was a clever general scholar and a good Irish one, and Mr. John Lloyd were charged by Messrs. O'Curry and O'Donovan with the fabrication of the inscription in the Ogham character on Mount Callan. On the other hand, the learned Dr. Ferguson has defended the genuineness of the inscription in a series of able papers read before the Royal Irish Academy.

The translation of the inscription by Professor O'Loony runs thus,

"Under this stone is laid Conaf [N] the fierce and turbulent."

LORD LECONFIELD AS AN IRISH LANDLORD.

Passing out of Quilty, a poor fishing village, we come upon a few admirably kept farms with ornamental homesteads; these are on the estate of Lord Leconfield, of Petworth, Sussex.

The skill and judgement with which his lordship's extensive Irish property is managed is a matter of just pride in the County Clare. The land is set on reasonable terms and all improvements requisite are first sanctioned and then executed under the directions of highly accomplished professional gentlemen acting for the landlord, the tenant being charged a moderate interest on the outlay.

Then we come to Annagh Bridge the scene of a tragic incident. The river itself from the bridge up to the mill may prove worth an artist's pilgrimage and reward a fisherman's skill. Looking under the lofty arch one has such a sweet sketch - a green patch and a many-coloured cliff in front, then the boulders and stream are beyond and all bounded by the tumbling surf outside.

The mill, too, is a picture, with the cascade over the rock. On the tall cliff grow the osmunda ferns. When the waters clear after a summer flood, the angler will meet white trout.

A BATHING-PLACE INDEED.

We are now in the sandhills and among the sweet, snug lodges of Milltown-Malbay, a bathing-place this, the very acme of halcyon bliss to quiet folk. Here the delicate juvenile, after pining in towns, and those wearied out with professional toils may bathe, and lounge and bathe again, and stretch on the sand, and, oh bliss supreme, be let alone, breathing the ozone and listening to the waves. Not but that postmen, butchers, bakers and vendors of all good things, from town and country, attend daily at the doors.

NIGHT FISHING.

And here, too, it is no small pleasure to embark in a canoe at the time of glowing sunset, when the Atlantic is all gold in the west, and to pass hour after hour of the mild, starry night, looking after the pollock or hovering on the edge of a scull of bream feeding on the flood-tide, and of course you lift them quite fast enough to keep yourself warm.

That fine old building in front is

which possesses ample accommodation and an excellent *cuisine*. The mansions around are chiefly of the Morony family.

THE GRAVES OF THE SPANIARDS.

That promontory on the left where the green wave swells so high, and its broken edge glitters so silvery bright in the sun, is Spanish Point. Just inside, at that rugged broken circle yonder, are the graves of the Spaniards. Traditions still live among the locals, some of them curious enough, concerning Boetius Clancy, of Knockfyne, head of an old stock and high sheriff of Clare, in the year of the great Armada wreck.

KILFARBOY.

By the way the parish is said by some to get its name from some such interment of dark-skinned strangers Kil-far-boy signifying, the Church of the Yellow-man. Mr. John Donovan, in his learned "Letters" considers the name to come rather from St. Fobrick, of whom nevertheless he gives but very little certain information. And now parting for awhile from our friends and leaving them to drive through Moy and Lahinch and on to their destination along a coast varying at every turn and bend, at every slope and swell, always deeply interesting and often extremely beautiful to the eyes of the lover of marine scenery, we return to

Limerick to convey some other friends less adventurous and less rewarded, who have preferred to run straight by the Limerick and Ennis Railway to their destination.

The Ennis Railway circles round a considerable portion of the north of Limerick City, and we cross the Shannon over an iron bridge intended for some Russian river. Some people always fidget on a bridge or in a viaduct. Whoever is not given to this weakness will look up the river; yes, from just half way across the bridge. There is a sweet rich scene for you, a perfect picture of its kind, and with such a rich, varied, deep-toned background. No terraces, no smoke of factories to spoil the effects. That church-spire is just in the right place, and underneath you the Shannon water is sparkling in floating threads of silvery eddies. The woods along the slopes towards which we are running are those of Cratloe, which Freney the robber haunted before he compounded and got a situation in the Customs at Waterford. On your right stands prettily over-hanging a mountain stream, Sixmile-Bridge, once having oil mills, &c.; its name arising from its having been counted six (old) miles from Limerick city by the mountain road. Here was a terrible election row, and blood, &c., flowing some twenty years ago. Elections recall to mind a curious account given by Mr. John O'Donohue in his History of the O'Briens of an election early in the last century.

We are now at the Ardsollus Station. Down on the left you find the Fergus on his way to the Shannon, and as you have moved a few perches onward, you will catch a glimpse of the chimneys of Dromoland Castle, seat of Lord Inchiquin, the representative of the kingly Celtic stock of Brian Borhoime. Here it was that, on September 5th, at Dromoland, 1776, the celebrated Arthur Young wrote one of his learned letters, rather indeed treatises, on the agriculture of the day. A note or two may amuse some readers - "Average rent in Co. Clare 5s. per acre, corcasses at 20s - rich meadow or fattening lands by the great rivers. Captain Tim McNamara farms 7000 acres, Mr. Singleton 4000. The tillage is carried on by little farmers. The course of crops - No. 1, potatoes, 2 bere, 3 wheat, 4 oats, 5 oats, 6 oats, 7 lay it out to grass. No. 2, another system of rotation - 1 beans, 2 bere, 3 barley, 4 wheat, 5 oats, 6 oats, 7 oats, 8 lay it out on beans again. (What will Scotch farmers with their rotations say to this? Doubtless that the soil is inexhaustible, or treated as such?) They fatten pigs on potatoes - but what much amazed me they fatten hogs on grass and make them as fat as bullocks. The poor make bread of beans; they prefer a bushel of them to a bushel of wheat. No clover is sown but by Sir L. O'Brien. Spinning is by no means general. The most profitable management of grazing is to buy in year-olds. Their average price is from £2 2s. to £2 10s. Their price, fat, at 4½ years old, is an average £8. Wool sells at 17s. 6d. a stone. 4000 bullocks are annually fattened in Clare; bought at

£6, sold at £10. 3000 Cows, bought at £3, sold at £5. 6000 fat wethers sold out of country annually at 20s. each. This country is famous for cyder orchards and the cakagee apple. Sir L. O'Brien expected a hogshead a tree from several." Relative to the Shannon, A. Young writes in glowing terms as he viewed it from Clonmelly Hill. "It is from one to three miles broad, a most noble river deserving regal navies for its ornament, or, what are better; fleets of merchant-men, the cheerful signs of far-extending commerce, instead of a few miserable fishing boats, the only canvas that swelled upon the scene. The whole view is magnificent."

QUIN ABBEY.

But if we turn our eyes the other way, there stands Quin Abbey yonder in the flat plain to the N. E. Oh, friend, if thy turn be contemplative, if thy mental training move in the sober pathways of Archæology pay a special visit to this most interesting relic of the past, the work of pious and generous devotion of the great Ma-cu-maras (= Son of the hound of the sea), a work wrought in stones, "quos non edax imber" - no, neither the pealing showers of the west, nor yet again, hostile fire, nor barbarian fury, have effaced or enfeebled their lingering lines of beauty. Yes, and here you will find the graves and inscriptions of many for some centuries past, of the MacCumaras, the O'Molonys, and others of the great Dalcassian stock of Thomond; and here too, of moderns, rests Fire Ball MacNamara and the titular bishop M'Mahon. It is a comfort to know that the

pile of skulls yonder in the corner for ay
diminishing, is now let alone, there being a general
return from the Scotch system of stimulating tillage
to the quiet old ways of pasturage.   But this
Ardsollas, or Hill of the Sun, was very famous in the
last century for races, which lasted for an entire
week in the year.

CLARE CASTLE.

Of Clare Castle we can only now mention that it is
a military station and has long been regarded of
great strategical value.   Lord Taaffe in an
unpublished letter, of date 16 August, 1646, thus
admonishes the careless, improvident governors: "I
am informed that you take but very little care or
regard to provide maintenance for the garrison I
appointed at Clare, whereat I may advertise your
being very sensible of the consequences therefrom.
Therefore I pray let not the said wardens have any
further cause of complaint in this particular,
otherwise you will hazard the securities of the said
place, whereby you may prejudice the public, and
specially incur the high displeasure of your very
loving friend - TAAFFE."

The old castle has a legend, - Mrs. Stamer,
daughter of William Yorke, the celebrated Limerick
Alderman, held her baby in arms while her husband
waited for the raising of the drawbridge. The baby
jumped from her arms into the rushing flood and
was lost. The shadowy form of a sad lady in white
rises from the river betimes and has scared and
disturbed   sentry   after   sentry.   Particular

...ns of this kind are made when the
...e changing quarters, at the same time it is
... noted that the men on such occasions take
...eeper drinks than usual in and out of the canteen.

Passing an old abbey we run into Ennis, once
called *"Innish Clonroad Ramfodha,"* or "the island of
the holm of the long rowing," and such it was
indeed up between the weary mud banks of the
Fergus. Ennis has been a borough since 1612.
Borough arms are a "field argent, three galleys with
their sails furled, sable." It has not been assaulted
or burned by any of the O'Briens since 1553.

Passing from the terminus one reaches the County
Jail, the neatness and order of which a distinguished
and popular writer has recently eulogised in
glowing terms. Less is known of the Old Jail, now
the Town Hall, in the street still called Jail-street. It
was here that the debtors used to be confined along
with the criminals, as every one knows from the
story of the Vicar of Wakefield; and from a bridge
spanning the street to afford extra jail
accommodation occasionally required in the
opposite house, the poor debtors used to drop down
by cords their hats and bags and earnestly
importuned cooked food from the charitable
passengers, which was then hauled up and
consumed. Humane provision was made by the old
Corporation of Ennis in their bye-laws for this class
of the community. "Light bread was to be sent to
such prisoners in her Majesty's (Queen Anne's)

gaole of the County of Clare as were declared paupers, and have not the Queen's allowance," also the bodies of "piggs and swine found straying in the streets and slain by the 'beadill' when not otherwise disposed of, viz., to the beadill himself."

THE BEGGARS OF ENNIS.

Mr. Thackeray some thirty years ago passed through Ennis and made his remarks upon this fraternity. How little he knew, good English soul, even though an Irishman wrote for him one or two of the best chapters of his "Irish Sketch Book," that the beggars of Ennis were an established institution. Yes; and, friend, while the horses are getting ready we prove this for you from the records of the Corporation on the subject. - In A.D. 1762 it is further provided "that no strolling beggar whatsoever shall go about begging in the Borough, except such as are lycensed (sic) by the Provost. And those so lycensed shall carry a badge to public view, with such stamp thereon as Provost shall think proper, and that Provost shall keep registry of such. N.B. - 6d. each to be allowed to 'Mace' for every such beggar brought before Provost."

THE ABBEY, - THE EDUCATION, - THE EMINENT MEN OF ENNIS.

The Franciscan Abbey of Ennis will well repay a visit. Its old east window deserves a place in the most recherè of sketch books. Indeed some other items of ecclesiastical construction and ornament are remarkably fine and need not special indication, as they tell their own story and commend themselves to the discerning; but, whatever else Ennis may be proud of, it is above all of the education and the genius of her sons. In the pre-reformation times the School of Clonroad was well-nigh as thronged with pupils and celebrated for progress as any of the other contemporaneous institutions of learning. In comparatively recent times, the following incidental allusion does rather convey a doubt of advanced intellectual culture being generally in the ascendant in Ennis - "The Court House is going to destruction occasioned by *public schools permitted to be kept there,* and by public exhibitions." This was in 1771; but the Erasmus Smith School had been set up through the active and enlightened zeal of Lord Chief Justice Marcus Patterson and Sir Lucius O'Brien, as executors of the will of Erasmus Smith, Esq. Lloyd gives an acrostic setting forth "the happy character" of this eminent legal gentleman, who did so much for his native town. This school sent to Trinity College, Dublin, Harte and Stephen Sandes, who both became Fellows, and a host of Scholars, Sizars and well-educated gentlemen. Indeed the Rev. Mr. Fitzgerald received a high expression of praise from the Lord Lieutenant of the day for his great success in the work of education. The Ennis College still retains its high character under the present Principal, Rev. F. E. Barnes; and there is another College too, very ably conducted, the Diocesan College. The Right Rev. Dr. Gregg, Bishop of Cork, is another of the sons of genius of whom Ennis is justly proud. Old Stephen O'Halloran taught him in his private school and many more. Dionysius

Lardner was another of the Ennis celebrities, and indeed Dion Boucicault's name may swell the list of them; also Mulready the great historical painter, whose house is still in the Causeway; and Dermody the poet; and Robert Crowe, M.P. who wrote against the Union and then voted for it; and Colonel O'Neill son of a tobacco twister, a man of lofty stature and noble bearing who volunteered and fought his way through the Peninsular Wars, up to the head of his regiment; also Chief Justice Patterson and Sir M. O'Loughlin, Master of the Rolls, were Ennis men; and the O'Gorman who wrote on fishing; and that wit of high renown, Giles Dixon, sent for by George IV. to crown his regal banquets with fascinating drollery. But as to the old Court House. This is all gone, and the site is marked now by the O'Connell statue. A handsome new Court House is now the field on which the ambition and eloquence of the modern Bar are displayed. If the "Irish forensic eloquence" of these times exceeds or equals that of John Philpot Curran, when "such a day came to be tried at Ennis by a special Jury the cause of Massey and Headfort," it is well done indeed.

And once more on the road to the west the eye is struck by the peculiar features of the great limestone field of North Clare - the rock being over instead of under the surface as is usual elsewhere; or, rather, more correctly speaking, there being rock without surface. The limestone field so fully developed in Lower Ormond reappears at Bodyke and runs on westward, through Tulla and Quin districts, by the north side of the Shannon, until from Ennis it takes a north-westerly line towards the coast, being bounded by the great coal-field which occupies the southern extremity of Clare.

And now we have slowly climbed Annuity Hill, so called by Giles Daxon on account of the grant for the reconstruction and repair of a road over it, made assizes after assizes, for many succeeding years.

DYSERT

What a rich, charming spot is Dysert, with the Hill overhanging on one side, and having Ballycullinan Lake on the other. No archæologist, no artist should pass it by. Here is the stump of a round tower still standing, and an antient cross repaired by the late F. H. Synge, Esq. The upper section of the erect shaft was nearly circular, just like the head of a man, and was held in equal esteem by the old women as an application for tooth-ache, and by the little boys as a very handy bowling-stone. In the church is an old Romanesque doorway, wonderfully preserved and of striking beauty. It is evidently nearly related to that in Killaloe Cathedral. It is depicted in "Towers and Temples of Ireland," and a photograph is promised in vol. ii. of Lord Dunraven's gorgeous "Notes, &c."

LAKE INCHIQUIN S. AND W.

Corofin offers not much for remark; but those who travel in a vehicle at their own command may, by a brief *detour*, pass along the southern and western shores of Inchiquin Lake greatly to their delectation. The scenery here and at Clifden House, also on the height from a huge rock at the road side, is of varied beauty. The beauty of hill and valley, of wood and water, of old, ivied castles, and quaint mills, with a vast prospect far away to the east bounded by mountains and rivers, and jemmed between with many a lake blue as the summer sky. As we emerge at the north-west angle is Crossard, or the Hill of the Cross, to which a learned writer refers as the boundary-stone or landmark of the Church-lands of St. Innewee, daughter of Boetius, after whom the parish is called Kilineboy, the other boundaries of the Termon being to the west at Elm Vale or Teigè-na-Croise, or "Cross," as is still called, and the third until recently standing on the Hill near the old gateway into Lemanegh. Mr. Dutton's sketch of the Cross and story of the affair are both pronounced erroneous and *absurd* by the learned author of "Letters," &c. But this last structure, whether intended to exhibit crossed hands or whatever else, has been removed. The socket is now empty; a Goth hath done this.

Killinaboy Church, at the foot of Roughan Hill, is in many respects remarkable. This Church of Innewee, thè daughter of Boetius (a name still locally given), has its walls in good preservation, measuring 62.8 x 20.3. There is a circular-headed doorway in south side, 13.6 from west gable and in dimensions 7.9 x 6.9, having the representation of a dwarf or stunted man on a stone over it in front. The author of "Towers and Temples," has some observations upon the peculiar significance of this and another figure in Dysert Church. Mr. John

O'Donovan pronounces "no part of the Church older than the 14th century except the west gable, which is of the 11th century. The monuments and inscriptions are to ordinary mortals the chief matters of interest. A circular low archway of stone marks the O'Quin resting-place.

O'FLANAGAN BODY AND BONES.

The O'Flanagan's tomb is elaborate. It exhibits a crucifixion and the two Marys, date 1644, and the following unique description:-

"Under these carvèd marbel stones
lyeth Conor O'Flanagan body and bones,
which monument was made by Anabel," &c.

ON HILLS TO BE SURMOUNTED.

But we must pass on from these charming lakes and churches, and castles, and cahirs, and legends, and all these fairy scenes, and commence the slow ascent of Roughan Hill. Doubtless such tracks were chosen in days when there was no carts and all transport was done by horses bearing burdens slung across their backs, and when the lowlands were flooded for the greater part of the year, or else heavy meadows covered them for the rest. This road runs on, hill over hill, until it approaches the gates of Lemanagh Castle, and passes between walls of great antiquity, overgrown with lichens well bleached.

ON RAILWAYS REQUIRED

But why there is not a railway does seem a strange thing. A railway was designed running from Ennis to Miltown by the flat lands of Inagh, but the project fell through, and the bill is withdrawn. Hopes are entertained that another effort may be made with better effect. From Ennis to Ruan, from Ruan to Corofin, in fact the whole way along the level of the Fergus valley, now smiling before us, and on to Kilfenora, four miles from Lisdoonvarna, and thence with a branch to Lisdoonvarna. The line might then run forward without much engineering difficulty, if not in the Lickeen at least in the Ballybreen valley direction, and by Ennistymon and Lahinch to Miltown Malbay.

ON SLOW COACHES STOPPING THE WAY.

There will be of course objections to this suggested line made by those who usually object to everything and accomplish nothing. But if Lisdoonvarna Spas be of such great medicinal value as the public incline to think, and agree to believe, it does seem a most curious fact, that a convenient and speedy mode of approach is not offered by those parties most concerned to advance the interests of the country and to consult for the wants of afflicted humanity. Would such spas, if to be found in England, Scotland or Wales, have been left so long in an almost unapproachable condition, at least approachable only by the very same roads in use over frightful "mountain tops ascending" for some decades of centuries past.

Facts are sometimes stranger than fiction itself. Lemanegh Castle stands in the midst of grass lands of extraordinary fertility. This was the residence of Colonel Connor O'Brien and his no less celebrated spouse Maureen Rhue, or Red Mary, of whom so many curious tales survive.

But there are other friends, not a few, who came by another route, and we attend upon these as before in the two other instances, and receive them at the borders of the county. The Midland Great Western Railway Company has made provision for those who would visit Lisdoonvarna by the Great Northern Route. These are passed across Galway Bay by steamer, land at Ballyvaughan, and ascend through the valley by a road well termed 'corkscrew,' until the great plateau of limestone is reached.

> "Where wilds immeasurably spread,
> Seem lengthening as we go,"

until at last Lisdoonvarna is reached by this third or northern approach.

CHAPTER II.

---◆---

ARRIVED at Lisdoonvarna, the visitor must needs look for accommodation in some of the hotels, lodging houses, or other available residences in the place, and accordingly a list of these is now given, particulars of course being stated by the parties on application or otherwise; and, indeed, much disappointment and discomfort will be saved by the visitor who is wise enough to write or wire beforehand and secure accommodation upon his arrival.

THE HOTELS

Although some have pronounced the "accommodation poor, defective, and very indifferent," and "that little can be said in praise of the Hotels," the man who cannot be pleased among the following Hotels, must be hard to please indeed.

1. THE EAGLE - founder, proprietor and manager, Mr. William Butler.

2. THE QUEEN'S HOTEL. This was founded by Mr. I. R. Annesley, and is now in the hands of a company, in which Mr. Annesley is a shareholder.

3. THE ROYAL HOTEL has been open since 1832. The proprietor is Mr. Ready.

4. THE IMPERIAL HOTEL is next to the Post Office. The proprietor is Mr. P. O'Dwyer, Ennistymon.

5. THE ATLANTIC HOTEL, proprietor, Mr. O'Brien, stands detached.

Of LODGING HOUSES there are several, indeed almost every house in Lisdoonvarna not a Hotel is a Lodging House. A few of these may be named - Miss Nolan's Lodging House at Rooska, also houses kept by Messrs. Markham, Lynch, Kennane, Mooney, &c. There is also Summer Hill, Mr. Coyne's House, and others.

Of PRIVATE VILLAS there are a few, which may be taken by the month or season; but parties will consult their own interest by looking after these themselves or by competent friends, and above all in good time before the hurry of the season has commenced.

Of FOOD none need fear a deficient supply or one of an inferior quality, or "carry with them provisions," as has been gravely suggested. Every day the best beef and mutton is killed; indeed the district is famous for its fattening qualities. Bread and groceries may also be had in the shops, fruit and vegetables are to be had too. The country and coast people supply in great abundance potatoes, eggs, milk, also fowl and fish; delicious Poldoody oysters may be had by those who can afford expensive luxuries.

THE POSTAL ACCOMMODATION is here copied as set forth in the April number of *British Postal Guide* and the Time Bill. Lisdoonvarna is a sub-office of Ennis; it is marked as a Money Order Office, and a Post Office Savings Bank, also as Postal Telegraph Office. A royal mail car runs daily, starting from Ennis, 4.45 a.m., and arriving at Lisdoonvarna at 8.45 a.m. The distance by the postal route is 25 English miles, and

the time allowed including stoppages is 3h. 50m.
The return car is despatched at 3.50 p.m., and
arrives in Ennis at 7.40. In Ennis the delivery begins
at 8.10, and at the same time a despatch takes place
of letters &c., to Dublin, England, and all parts of
Ireland, except portions of Co. Galway." There are
two

PLACES OF WORSHIP

in the village. A very small structure was built to
accommodate the visitors of the Protestant
Episcopal Church some years ago. This being
inadequate is to be superseded immediately by a
large and handsome building. There is also a
Roman Catholic Chapel.

As to the TOPOGRAPHY of the village, Lisdoonvarna
is situated in the barony of Burren, and in the parish
of Kilmoon, and is called after the townland on
which it stands. In "The Book of Survey and
Distribution" this is denominated "Lisdoonvarna
and Balleighteig, arable and pasture, pasturable and
mountain, and the parties for whom the grants held
good were John Sarsfield, the Earl of Inchiquin, St.
James Galway, Cyprian Devereux, Mary Burke,
Doctor Madden, Teige Ryan, and Pierce Creaghe."

The present owners in fee are Capt. Wm.
Stacpoole, M.P., Ennis, as representative of Edward
Hogan, Esq.; Pierce Creaghe, Esq., representative of
the original grantee, whose property in Co. Limerick
was taken from him, and equivalents in Co. Clare
substituted. This is set forth in the Acts of Settlement
and Explanation, also in a very curious complaint

engraved in the elaborate Creaghe family tomb, still standing in the Franciscan Abbey, Ennis. The other proprietors are James O'Brien, Esq., Ballinalacken, and the representative of Joseph Gore, Esq., of Derrymore. The properties run into close points of contact here. Those who read of "the opposed interests of the two principal proprietors standing in the way of general measures being adopted," will form an erroneous conclusion as to the cause of the unfinished state of Lisdoonvarna. This arises simply from the fact of the place having suddenly outgrown itself. The present village was not the original Lisdoonvarna. The remains of this are not quite gone. About a mile on the Ennis road, near a bridge, one turns sharply to the left and comes to a homestead, with traces of a grand terraced garden wall. Here was the home of the O'Daverens, one of the old clans. Mr. John O'Donovan relates that tradition has handed down the memory of this family in not a pleasing light, and among other qualities, tells of their being of the "true game cock breed." This however might be of rather general application among the old Celtic families. But the castle has disappeared, and there are some traces in ruins of the residences of Mr. E. Hogan, and others.

But "over there," sir, is the *Lis*, said the "genius Loci," and he was right. That round green hill, or *Lis*, once had a *Dun* or fort on it, and still stands at a "*bhearna*," or gap between the hills; and this accounts for the name of the now celebrated village of Sulphur and other Spas - Lis-doon-varna. And it was near this also there stood the small village to which allusion is made in the following receipt from the Collector of Hearth-money, the original being before us:-

"TOWN OF LISDOONVARNA - Received from Edmond Hogan, Esquire, the sum of 16s., due to His Majesty for 8 Hearths, payable 10th day of January, 1748, I say received, this 4th day of October, 1749, by me. - JOHN CAMAC."

This locality is marked by a total absence of trees; indeed trees have no place to put their roots into in the limestone formation at least; also there are at close intervals valleys and slopes among the hills which seem cut into watercourses, all generally taking a direction more or less westerly towards the Atlantic.

The great limestone field here comes in contact with the superincumbent shale, and no doubt can be but that these conditions have considerably influenced the temperature of Lisdoonvarna.

The land breezes coming off the grey bare wastes of limestone considerably warmed, as the hand may test by contact with the heated surface of sun-scorched rock, and then meeting the sea breezes laden with moisture and enlivened with ozone of the Atlantic about three miles distant, both combine to form that balmy, refreshing and delicious air which none can breathe without exquisite gratification and the cultivation of a prodigious appetite. The sanitary state of the village is now carefully attended to under the new laws which are administered with vigour and intelligence.

stands, or rather stood, in the townland of Kilmoon; walls 52 by 18; all its features are destroyed. There is a stone near exhibiting a mitred head supposed to represent that of St. Mugdanus, Bishop of Errigal. Near hand is a standing stone called the Cross. There is another well in the townland of Lisdoonvarna dedicated to St. Brendan.

The Cahirs, or great circular stone forts, in this immediate parish are not conspicuous.

Mr. J. O'Donovan refers to a remarkable round hill called Lisatseeaun, or the Fort of the Fairies. But fear not, thou gentle stranger, for these tshee, or fairies, are not demons or fallen angels but good people - the spirits of the Tuath-a-Danaan, and of some of the Milesian tribes whom they have spirited away to live with them in the mysterious recesses of those sweet green pillows of dreaming.

The great limestone field which spreads across the whole north of Clare, or Burren, running continuously from the east at Bodyke, as mentioned, takes a more decided north-westerly direction from Inchiquin, and is met by the superincumbent shales at this place, at Kilfenora and at Lisdoonvarna. The Memoirs of Geological Survey, by the late F. J. Foot, Esq., refer to the Kilfenora and Lisdoonvarna districts in the following terms:-

GEOLOGY OF THE KILFENORA AND LISDOONVARNA DISTRICTS.

"The village of Kilfenora stands on a flat formed of the uppermost beds of the limestone, and enclosed

38

on the north-west and south by the superincumbent coal measure shales which form high ground.

"The limestone is nearly horizontal, or dips gently north and south at 2° or 3°.

"Along the boundary line or escarpment are many exposures of the shales, and sometimes they are seen in conjunction with the limestone. The best sections are in the bed of the stream on the east side of Tullagh Fort, one mile east-south-east of Kilfenora, near the road, south-west of Fanta Glebe-house, in the stream-course a quarter of a mile north of Ballyshanny House, where they may be plainly seen resting on the limestone, both abounding in fossils."

For the vertical section at the place the reader is referred to the original work.

"There is also a good junction, showing a nearly similar section, in the stream course at the west side of the road, about one third of a mile north-west of Lismoher House. But in no part of the district, or, perhaps indeed, in no other part of Ireland, is the junction between the two formations so beautifully exhibited and on such a large scale as in the numerous ravines about Lisdoonvarna, in many of which the observer may walk for miles in dry weather, having beneath his feet the uppermost bed of the limestone, and on each side of him perpendicular walls of shale.

"It is along this junction that the Spa Wells, for which Lisdoonvarna is celebrated, occur."

In one of these ravines behind the Eagle Hotel there used to lie, strewed about in wild confusion, several fine fossils of the class *reptilia* and order *chelonia* or tortoise. One very large specimen remains still. Of those seen some were broken across in a vertical section, doubtless by the action of the torrents, and the yellow fat and green flesh are plainly indicated. "Centuries and thousands of years," writes Buckland, the father of geology, "may have rolled away between the time in which these footsteps were imprinted by tortoises upon the sands of their native land and the hour when they are again laid bare and exposed to our curious and admiring eyes. Yet we behold them stamped upon the rock distinct as the track of the passing animal upon the recent snow, as if to show that thousands of years are but as nothing amidst eternity, and as it were in mockery of the fleeting, perishable course of the brightest potentates, and of mankind." - *Bridgewater Treatise*.

Searching for these fossils and their indelible tracks, both in this stream and in other neighbouring rivulets of which notice has been given, the visitor will find a healthful and instructive pastime, but this must be only in dry weather.

P. D.

CHAPTER III.

———◆———

THE SPAS OF LISDOONVARNA.

THE TWIN SPAS

By means of the Parliamentary grant for Scientific Reports, the Royal Irish Academy enabled Mr. Plunkett, F.C.S., Assistant Chemist in the Royal College of Science, and Mr. Studdert, LL.D., Ex-Sch. T.C.D., to examine these mineral waters at the Springs and in the Laboratory. Their Report was read by Mr. Plunkett, May 24, 1875, before the Academy. The following are extracts from it, as printed in the Transactions :-

"Before proceeding to Lisdoonvarna the authors procured a jar of the principal sulphur water of the place, which was carefully collected from the Gowlaun Well, through the aid of

Dr. Cullinan, of Ennis; of this preliminary examination was then made.

"In August they visited Lisdoonvarna in order to determine at the springs the sulphuretted hydrogen that might have escaped, and the iron that might have become peroxidised before reaching Dublin; and also for the purpose of procuring a large supply of the waters, to determine their more stable constituents. This lengthened investigation the authors were permitted by Professor Galloway to conduct in the laboratory of the Royal College of Science, Stephen's Green, Dublin, with all appliances available.

"Remaining at Lisdoonvarna until the 5th of September, they repeatedly estimated at the well itself the sulphuretted hydrogen in the Gowlaun Spring, and in a secondary one near the east end of the parish Church. They also then determined the iron present as protoxide in the principal, and in the secondary chalybeate well, both situated at Rathbawn Bridge.

"It may be right (as the authors said), to remark that there are no interments in the churchyard; that spring there issues from the cliff-side, and is one of a pair of spas, sulphur and iron, in one recess, and nearly joining at their mouths, thence called the 'Twin Spas.' The iron one was not flowing then.

"The *temperature* (which is said to be equable) of the *two sulphur* and *two iron spas* was ascertained as compared with that of the atmosphere; also the rate of flow of the 'Twin Sulphur Spring;' but the underground position of the springs at Gowlaun and Rathbawn prevented their rate of flow being determined. However, notwithstanding their many drinkers, the level of these two principal wells is said to be rather constant.

"The explanations to accompany Sheets 114, 122, and 123 of the maps of the Geological Survey of Ireland, illustrating parts of the Counties of Clare and Galway, by Mr. Frederick J. Foot, M.A., give the geological formation of the Lisdoonvarna district, which may account for the nature of its springs. At page 27, Mr. Foot observes that 'Iron occurs in the form of iron-stone nodules and thin bands in the shales about

42

Lisdoonvarna . . . . also as iron pyrites, with the crystals of which mineral (he adds) the black fissile shales, when they are unweathered, may be seen coated.' He seems correct in remarking (page 28) that 'It is from the decomposition of the iron pyrites [sulphide of iron] in the coal measures, that these wells [at Lisdoonvarna] derive their sulphur and iron.'

"It may be added, in passing, that Mr. Foot gives a correct wood-cut of the 'Twin Spas' as Figure 9 of his report.

"Following the suggestion of recent eminent writer, from a medical point of view, on these and other spas of Ireland (Dr. Mapother) who advised lithia to be looked for in the Gowlaun water, the authors made that search by means of the spectroscope, and the *presence of lithium* (by the position of its distinctive crimson band) *was ascertained*. This constituent seems to have been detected in this water now for the first time. Dr. Mapother relies on it as a curative agent of much value.

"Another medical gentleman, Mr. William Faussett, M.B., F.R.C.S., who visited Lisdoonvarna in 1867, as he says, 'for his own health's sake,' states, in an account of his visit (page 13), that 'The sulphur and chalybeate springs of Lisdoonvarna when judiciously used, and supplemented as occasion, in some cases, may require, possess an extensive range of therapeutical action; and being free from the excess of any irritating ingredients, such as common salt, will, on this account, be found more beneficial than spas which have hitherto been held in higher repute.'

GOWLAUN SULPHURETTED HYDROGEN WELL.

"The temperature of this water, as drawn from the well, was found to be 11°C., (= 51.8°F.) the air at the time being 15.5°C. It contains, in addition to the usual constituents of well water, 5.553 cubic centimetres of sulphuretted hydrogen in the litre. The unoxidized sulphur exists entirely combined with hydrogen. It also contains, as before mentioned, traces of *lithium*. The following table gives the quantities of the several constituents:-

	Parts in one million	Grains in one gallon
Silica	13.6	.952
Sulphuric acid, calculated as SO$_4$	10.0	.700
Chlorine	29.6	2.072
Lime precipitated on boiling, calculated as Ca	35.0	2.450
Lime retained in solution on boiling, calculated as Ca	2.7	.189
Magnesia precipitated on boiling, calculated as Mg	17.1	1.197
Magnesia retained in solution on boiling, calculated as Mg	1.4	.098
Lithium	Traces	Traces
Soda, calculated as Na	61.9	4.333
Potash, " K	3.0	.210

Which may be calculated as being in combination thus :-

Silica	13.6	.952
Calcic carbonate	87.5	6.125
Magnesic "	60.1	4.207
Sodic "	102.3	7.161
Calcic sulphate	8.1	.567
Magnesic "	6.0	.420
Sodic chloride	44.4	3.108
Potassic "	5.7	.399
	327.7	22.939
Sulphuretted hydrogen	c.c. per litre 5.553	

The specific gravity referred to water at 15° C. was 1.0006.

RATHBAWN CHALYBEATE WELL.

"The temperature of this water was found to be 13°C. (=55.4° F.) when that of the air was 15.1°C., being a difference of only 2.1°, whilst in the case of the Gowlaun water, the difference was 45°: this may be accounted for by the open situation of this well, which is more freely exposed to sunshine. This water contains, in addition to the usually occurring substances, a ferrous salt, and also a *weighable quantity of manganese*; this latter substance does not appear to have been before detected. The several constituents are:-

	Parts in one million	Grains in one gallon
Silica	12.1	.847
Sulphuric acid, calculated as SO_4	124.7	8.729
Chlorine	35.5	2.485
Iron, calculated as Fe	17.1	1.197
Manganese " Mn	0.8	.056
Lime precipitated on boiling, calculated as Ca	56.0	3.920
Lime retained in solution on boiling, calculated as Ca	24.8	1.736
Magnesia precipitated on boiling, calculated as Mg	2.7	.189
Magnesia retained in solution on boiling calculated as Mg	16.8	1.176
Soda calculated as Na	20.5	1.435
Potash calculated as K	2.5	.175

Which may be calculated as being in combination thus :-

Silca	12.1	.847
Ferric oxide, with trace of alumina	2.7	.189
Ferrous carbonate	31..7	2.219
Manganous "	1.7	.119
Calcic "	140.0	9.800
Magnesic "	9.5	.665
Calcic sulphate	84.3	5.901
Magnesic "	84.0	5.880
Sodic chloride	52.1	3.647
Potassic "	6.4	.448
	424.5	29.715

The specific gravity referred to water at 15°C. was 1.0006.

"In the same enclosure with the last mentioned, is another chalybeate, known as the Magnesian iron water. As it has now fallen into disuse, it did not seem necessary to do more than determine the iron which it contains. Calculated as carbonate, it was 14.9 mgr. per litre, or 1.043 grains per gallon.

"Of that remarkable pair the 'Twins,' only one - the sulphur spring - was flowing; it is essentially of the same character as the Gowlaun water. It contains 2.052 cub. cent. sulphuretted hydrogen per litre. The temperature was 11.6°C. (= 52.9°F.) the air being 15.4° C. The rate of flow was found to be one litre discharged in one minute and twenty seconds, or about ten gallons in one hour."

What is new and most important in the foregoing analyses is the discovery of LITHIUM in the *sulphur spring*, and MANGANESE in the *chalybeate spring*. No spa in the United Kingdom is reported to contain either of these combinations, save a Manganese "*trace*" found by Dr. Hofmann in Harrowgate water.

Lithium, but not *Manganese,* is valuable in quantities *not* weighable. The *only sulphur spring* on the Continent of Europe with LITHIUM present is *Weilbach,* in Nassau. Mr. Squire's Companion to the British Pharmacopæia, (10th edition p. 348), gives Fresenius' Analysis for Weilbach water, reporting its temperature at 57°F, but little over that of the Gowlaun water. The local Guide Book reports it "good in chest diseases, in gout, rheumatism, and herpetic affections." It contains the other constituents of the Gowlaun Spa.

It will also be seen from the analysis of *Rathbawn* chalybeate, that MANGANESE is present as well as IRON. The *Companion to the Pharmacopœia* gives from the Analyses by Chemists and the Guide Books, some similar approved spas on the Continent. For instance, Alexisbad and Alexisbrunnen, in Germany, two miles from Harzgerode. Altwasser, in Prussian Silesia. At Baden-Baden, the Hauptquelle; and with Lithium in the Murquelle and Fettquelle. These two are called *"the Lithia water for gout and lithiasis."* At Bagneres-de-Luchon, in the south of France, IRON and MANGANESE are together present in the water, which is said to be "good in lymphatic and cutaneous affections." Again, at Carlsbad in Bohemia *these* are found together *with Lithium*: this water is "drunk for obstinate constipation, affections of the liver, gout, rheumatism, and diabetes." IRON and MANGANESE are reported present at Ems: and with LITHIUM also at Frazenbad, in Bohemia, in five wells, at a temperature varying from 51°F. to 54°F. These are reported "highly successful in all forms of

47

abdominal plethora, anæmia and chlorosis." At Gastein, in Austria, MANGANESE and IRON are combined; and at Frankenheil, in Bavaria, where the water is said to be "useful in scrofulous diseases of the skin;" and at Kronthal, in Nassau, said to be "resorted to by persons suffering from bronchitis, or affections of the lungs:" the temperature of the two wells there is 57°F. and 61°F. Also at Landeck, in Prussian Silesia; and at Marienbad, in Bohemia, IRON and MANGANESE with *Lithium* are reported to be in three wells, their temperature varying from 44°F. to 54°F. It is stated that these "springs are used as laxatives, and are useful in abdominal enlargement, gravel, gout, and derangement of the digestive organs;" also that "mud baths are applied to stimulate the skin, and to remove glandular swellings." At Orezza, in Corsica, the water at 59°F. contains IRON and MANGANESE, and is said to be "drunk with benefit for indigestion, want of appetite, and general debility." Also at Saint Maurice, in the Upper Engadine, Switzerland, the water at 42°F. contains IRON and MANGANESE, and is reported as "tonic and stimulating in debility, anæmia, neuralgia, scrofula, and in some conditions of lung diseases." Also at Schwalback, in Nassau, said to be "resorted to for quiet , and recruiting dilapidated health." Of two wells here, the Stahlbrunnen, temp. 46°-51°, is "drunk for general torpidity." The Seidlitz water in Bohemia; and the Seltzers in Nassau, contain both IRON and MANGANESE. Also the water of Toeplitz, in Bohemia; and that of Vals, in France, *along with* LITHIUM (*trace*), temp. 66°F. to 68°F; this latter is reported "beneficial in *Lithiasis, indigestion, and skin diseases."*

The Vichy Water (France) contains a *trace* of MANGANESE, with IRON. The water at Weisbaden, in Nassau, contains LITHIUM along with MANGANESE and IRON. And the Wildbad water in Würtemburg contains IRON and MANGANESE.

These chalybeates contain the other constituents of the Rathbawn well.

It will be seen in the *Pharmacopœia* that IRON and MANGANESE combined are prescribed by the Faculty. We have seen such a *recipe* from Dr. A. Hudson of Merrion-square, Dublin. A Cheltenham physician of eminence, it appears, administers the combination as *"a tonic and alterative."*

L. S.

———————

CHAPTER IV.

------◆------

The design of this chapter is to lay before the profession and the public the results of five years' continued and rather extensive investigation of the effects of Lisdoonvarna Spas upon different classes of disease.

It is considered that this object may be best accomplished by stating *seriatim* the diseases which have been brought under spa-treatment, together with the results obtained.

ARTHRITIC DISEASES.

In gout the sulphur has had a decidedly good effect. A large number of cases has been treated, and not one has been noticed in which more or less benefit was not derived. The majority of these were chronic cases. It must not be supposed, however, that all cases of gout benefit in an equal degree, so much being dependent upon the habits of the individual. It is notorious that gouty subjects are partial to the pleasures of the table, and are particularly addicted to the eating and drinking of those articles which are most injurious to them. We have often been surprised at seeing those who had come to Lisdoonvarna to be cured by the use of the Spa defeat this object by indulging in viands so poisonous to a gouty system, as lobster, salmon and champagne. It is not to be wondered at, then, that persons who act in this manner do not improve as those improve who are careful in the selection of their diet.

Rheumatism.-Acute Rheumatism (Rheumatic fever) during its febrile stages is not a disease which admits of spa-treatment. And no such cases have been presented; but we have had many cases in the convalescent stages in which the good effect of the sulphur-water of Lisdoonvarna is even more marked than in gout. There was not a single patient who did not derive considerable benefit, amounting in many cases to an apparently perfect recovery. Some, who, on their arrival at Lisdoonvarna were unable to move without help, and were affected moreover with cardiac complications, in two or three weeks were able to walk about freely, while the heart symptoms were considerably ameliorated. The patients themselves expressed the greatest satisfaction at the relief obtained. We have in our recollection a peculiar instance of a young person who, after Rheumatic fever, suffered under a severe attack of genuine gout, and the improvement gained after a fortnight's use of the Spa was truly surprising.

Chronic Rheumatism and Rheumatoïd Arthritis (Rheumatic Gout).-A vast number of patients suffering from these allied complaints in some of their forms resorts to Lisdoonvarna. Generally speaking, we may see that the majority of them have been benefited thereby. The amount of improvement depends upon the length of time through which the disease had worked, or the intensity of its action. Persons whose joints are become "anchylosed" or whose "synovial fluid" has dried up, cannot expect that a course of sulphur or any other water will restore them to full activity of their limbs. But the majority of this class of patients really do admit that they have become better able to move about than they were formerly, also that their pains are less troublesome. It may be well to mention that a few complain of an accession of stiffness and pain after they have drunk the water for some days, and of these some get disheartened at this, thinking that the Spa does not suit their case, and it requires persuasion to induce such persons to prolong their stay for a sufficient time. Here we may observe that a sojourn of two or three weeks is not at all sufficient for these chronic cases. Such patients should make arrangements to remain for five or six weeks at least, in order to derive any substantial and permanent benefit. A good division of the time for these would be that they pay a first visit in the earlier and a second in the later part of the seasons, allowing an interval of some three of four months.

DISEASES OF THE ORGANS OF DIGESTION.

Dyspepsia. - This very common, and often intractable, ailment arises from so many and differing causes, and manifests its existence in so many forms as well as degree of intensity, that it must be understood that the principles of treatment vary considerably. There is no complaint which exhibits such varying results from Spa-water or any other treatment. One or another of the Spas may agree remarkably well with one person, while none of them can be tolerated by another person. Again, considerable judgement must be exercised in the prescription of the water suitable to each individual. Some patients can only tolerate very small doses at a time; for others one moderate dose in the day suffices, while a third class cannot take any Spa whatsoever. These last, accordingly must look for an improvement of their ailment rather from rest, recreation and plenty of good air. We may say that the iron-water, unless otherwise contra-indicated, is generally the most suitable to the ordinary atonic Dyspepsia of persons leading a sedentary life; at the same time, individuals of this class who are inclined to a plethoric habit, in fact who may have too much blood to manage well, must not attempt to take the iron-water unless it has been particularly prescribed; the neglect of this precaution has attended with very serious results. Having now given the warning, we proceed to state that in many cases the beneficial action of the Spa that is ordered may be decidedly advanced by the use, under advice, of an appropriate drug.

Under this head it may be noted that the very few cases in which simple enlargement of the spleen was diagnosed, derived much benefit from the use of the Iron Spa.

DERANGEMENTS OF THE LIVER.

Omitting all details about serious cases of organic disease, we now refer only to those for which the use of Spa-water may be contemplated. These latter are chiefly convalescents from jaundice and sufferers from the ordinary torpid liver, attended with the usual symptoms. In both of these complaints the use of the sulphur Spa has been attended with happy results. However, as this water, unlike that of Harrowgate, possesses no aperient ingredient, it is generally advisable that the patient use some corrective, such as citrate of magnesia, Rochelle salt, Frederickshall water, &c.

The sulphur Spa has been found exceedingly beneficial in hoemorrhoidal affections, especially if used as an adjunct to the usual remedies which had proved ineffective without the Spa.

Entozoa. - The sulphur-water has proved singularly effective in cases of *Lumbrici*. We have had no opportunities of observing whether it may be of equal efficacy in cases of *Taenia* or *Ascarides*.

DISEASES OF THE RESPIRATORY ORGANS.

The sulphur Spa has proved of marked efficacy in all the cases coming under observation of chronic irritability of the mucous membrane of the throat and larynx. As to Bronchitis, it need hardly be stated that, in its acute form this disease does not properly come under Spa-treatment; but there are cases of chronic bronchial affections for which the Spa may be recommended. In ordinary cases which are attended with copious expectoration, but unaccompanied by serious structural changes in the lung-tissue, the sulphur-water has been used with advantage. But we have found that the progress of

54

these cases has been greatly influenced by the state of the weather prevalent during the sojourn of the patient at Lisdoonvarna, fine weather greatly enhancing the beneficial action of the Spa, cold and wet counteracting it seriously.

As to Pneumonia and Pleurisy in convalescent stage, persons recovering from the acute attacks of the above generally make a rapid and complete recovery at Lisdoonvarna; but this is not less due to the pure fresh air than to the use of any of the waters.

As to Phthisis, we do not at all recommend Lisdoonvarna as a fit resort for consumption. The Spas are useless, and the air in the very best state of weather is too strong for them, while in the wild and wet storms to which this coast is liable, a continuance in the locality is most injurious.

As to Asthma, notwithstanding the favourable opinions which have been expressed by some authorities, based chiefly on theories of the efficacy of sulphur in asthmatic affections, we must confess that, out of a good many cases of this complaint sent to Lisdoonvarna, we have never observed any improvement gained: on the contrary, many patients had to leave the place soon after their arrival, the disease becoming greatly aggravated, even independently of the state of the weather.

NEPHRITIC AND VESICAL DISEASES.

A few cases of Bright's disease in the chronic form were treated, and derived some benefit from the judicious use of the iron-water. In Diabetes mellitus the use of the sulphur Spa originated from observations of a case in which, an ignorant person, of his own accord, and in the simple confidence of the all-curing powers of the Spa, found benefit. The treatment, though apparently hazardous, after this was tried under medical advice with the frequent result of a mitigation of the prominent symptoms. And some confidence exists as to its comparative efficacy.

In the class of cases in which the diathesis of uric acid exists, the use of the sulphur Spa is unquestionably beneficial; but in cases of other kinds of deposit this has not been found of such marked benefit.

CUTANEOUS DISEASES.

Very many persons labouring under this complaint resort to Lisdoonvarna yearly, although the varieties of the complaints themselves are somewhat limited. A large number of patients suffering from the very common disease of eczema come from relief. The results of the treatment of this disease are as follows:-

When the sulphur Spa alone was used nothing very encouraging appeared; however, on a more extended experience of the administration of the water in each individual case, results were exhibited which were most satisfactory; and we feel bound to say, that appropriate local treatment was attended in many cases, with advantage. In psoriasis, the use of the sulphur-water is attended with various results; some cases yielding to it - others not; those that are recent being more amenable, as might be expected. In acne, the result of treatment by spa has proved generally good. One well-marked case of pityriasis rubra (a rather rare disease) was dealt with, and the result of treatment was very favourable.

<h2 style="text-align:center">SCROFULOUS COMPLAINTS.</h2>

In a scrofulous state of the systems, the iron spa is beneficial, though it may be necessary in some cases to precede the use of this water by a short course of sulphur.

<h2 style="text-align:center">AFFECTIONS OF THE NERVOUS SYSTEM.</h2>

Neuralgia. - The cases of neuralgia in the face and head were decidedly benefited by the use of the iron spa. Lumbago and sciatica, also appear to be favourably influenced by the use of this water, except in those cases depending upon a rheumatic taint, in which sulphur is obviously indicated. Paralysis, the only kind in which we had an opportunity for testing spa-treatment, was known to medical men as locomotor ataxy; here we can only say, that any improvement was made rather in the general state of the health than in the disease itself.

<h2 style="text-align:center">DOSE OF THE SPA.</h2>

Although so many persons expect that they ought to get definite information on this point from a guide-book, we consider it necessary to lay it down emphatically, that it would be impossible to do this. The doses of the different spas require to be regulated according to the age, sex, constitution of the patient, and nature of disease, - just like any other medicinal agent. We have seen a vast amount of injury follow the neglect of this. Persons suffering from the very different maladies, thinking that one system of *doseage* is applicable to all. We may state, that the doses vary from one table-spoonful to over half-a-gallon per diem.

BATHS

The baths at Lisdoonvarna comprise at present cold and warm, reclining and shower-baths; either of ordinary or of sulphur spa water supplied from a spring on the premises. Acid, alkaline, or other medicated baths can be supplied, if prescribed. Under this head we append a few remarks upon the use of natural sulphur-water externally. While popular ideas go strongly in the side that the baths of the sulphur spa ought to cure all cutaneous and every other disease besides. On the other hand, medical authorities incline rather to think that the power to be justly expected from such curative applications is but insignificant, owing to the fact that the special curative agent being in solution in so small a degree. As an illustration of the lengths to which the latter class of opinion has gone, we note the argument used by Dr. Julius Brown[1].

---

[1] See book II., ch. iv., "On the Curative Effects of Baths and Waters," translated by Dr. Herman Weber. Smith, Elder, & Co. : London, 1875.

We are not disposed to agree with either of these extreme views, while we do not attribute too much to external application of sulphur spa for curing everything, neither do we incline to the view that it is quite inert. Our reasons for this cannot here be given. From our own experience of the spa water baths, we think that it is a potent agent for good, or the reverse. We have not the least doubt but that a portion of the sulphuretted hydrogen is absorbed into the system through the skin, as well as through the lungs which receive the air impregnated with the gas. Moreover, many patients suffering from chronic rheumatic affections, who had been in the habit of visiting Lisdoonvarna for years before the baths were opened, and trusted solely to the drinking of the spas, found that the baths considerably strengthen and hasten forward the effects obtained through the internal use of the waters. On the other hand, we are not at all so sanguine as to the beneficial effects of the bath in skin diseases. We had to disuse them in exematous affections, the water seeming to act as an irritant in a way such as ordinary water does not act. In squamous skin diseases, they appear to be inert; while in "acne," for which the external use of sulphur is an established remedy, we have not found them powerful enough, and I have been obliged to superadd sulphur artificially.

We bring these observations to a close by some

such as should be followed by patients undergoing a course of mineral waters.

In this respect, the hotel and lodging-house proprietors have much to learn before their management of the house and of the table can be looked upon with approval, as suitable to invalids. Of persons in robust health, who require little extra trouble, we don't speak. But the delicate attentions and the special administrations which invalids require, must not be despised or thought over-troublesome to the parties concerned, when they consider the large number of such invalids resorting to the place and making their care so remunerative. Indeed, so important is this point, that we do not hesitate to make known the fact that, in Germany - which may be regarded as the very cradle and home of scientific spa treatment - the medical man is really made *the King of the Kitchen,* and his word is law, as to the general as well as to the particular diet for all under medical treatment, whether their cases be slight or severe. We hardly expect that such a system could be worked out in Lisdoonvarna; but, certainly, the simple joint is better than the ill-concocted attempt at a French dish; and a good carver, with a dinner laid out *a la Russe,* will prove at once far more comfortable to the guests, and even more economical to the *Maitre d'Hotel.* Such a system may be of advantage even to the robust, who, perhaps, may be hungry, and yet do not like to exhibit a voracious forwardness at the table. At the same time, it is possible that Lisdoonvarna may yet progress in such a way, that invalids may find houses, and systems of management, and a dietary specially prepared for them, and calculated to afford them that quiet and comfort which conduce so largely to their perfect restoration to health. Quiet and social out-door recreations may also be encouraged; but the getting up of these will depend greatly upon the visitors themselves.

S. W.

CHAPTER V.

---◆---

EXCURSIONS FROM LISDOONVARNA

IN reference to drives from Lisdoonvarna, it may suffice to remark in general that those who desire this kind of exercise and enjoyment, have an abundant supply of vehicles always available, from the stately drag and the sociable long car down to the swaying gingle with the jibbing horse, so proudly and fondly addressed as "Telegraph" by his artful master on the box.

THE FIRST EXCURSION

may be taken to the Cliffs of Moher.

THE CLIFFS OF MOHER

The form of the ground in the way of general description is thus given in Geological Survey of Clare: "To the north of Liscannor Bay, in the promontory of Hag's Head the ground also rises to heights of 500 and 600 feet, especially along the coast, which exhibits a line of magnificent precipices nearly three miles long, and rising at one part quite perpendicularly to a height of 668 feet. These form the well-known Cliffs of Moher. The almost continuous section along the coast exhibits the structure of the whole district West of Lisdoonvarna, the beds of limestone and superincumbent shales, which northwards occur at a height of more than 1000 feet above the sea, are brought by the southerly dip to the sea level, and as we go south along the coast, higher and higher beds are seen. The basal shales, here about 80 feet in thickness, pass upwards into sandy flags; and about three quarters of a mile from Fisherstreet, strong olive grits and flags may be seen at the top of the cliff, which is about 70 feet high, the beds dipping south-east at 5°. At Faunmore the shales and flags beneath these grits are curiously contorted, as if by some great lateral pressure, which did not effect the beds above or below them. These contortions may be seen for more than half a mile along the cliffs.

"A little south of Luogh Point, and less than one mile from Faunmore, the strong grits and flags which lately occupied the top of the cliff above the contorted shales, are brought by the southerly dip to the sea level at the base of the cliff, and above them are thick black shales, about 260 feet in thickness, or the same, as the height of the cliff, as the beds are nearly horizontal.

"Proceeding southward the cliffs increase in height, and at the top olive grey flags are seen resting on about 300 feet of shale. Further south-west are more flags above these, alternating with shale-bands; these are the track-marked flags previously mentioned. They are extensively quarried in this neighbourhood, and being easily worked, as the width of their joints renders them capable of being procured of any size, are in great demand. They are largely exposed in crags inland, in the townlands of Lough South and Caherbarnagh.

"Above these flags and forming the top of the cliffs of Moher, is a bed of black shale, more than 40 feet in thickness; this is the highest bed in the immediate district. Between the flags and this shale is a calcareous band from three to five inches in thickness full of fossils, and exhibiting in a beautiful manner the singular structure known as *cone-within-cone*. The axes of the cones are perpendicular to the planes of stratification. This band is traceable along the cliffs for upwards of a mile.

"From the Stokeen cliff the ground slopes gradually to Liscannor Bay. - At Hag's Head, in the shale beneath the flags, are numerous nodules and small grit bands.

"At Carrigatrial, at the foot of the cliff, and among the great masses of debris fallen from above, stems of plants and ferns were observed, as also fragments of calc-spar with small pieces of coal. South of

64

Moher House the seam of coal is traceable for nearly half a mile, the dip being south from 5° to 15°."

To get into the best position for a thorough ocular examination of the geological character of the cliffs of Moher, the direct road from Lisdoonvarna is not the most desirable; one must rather approach by Doolin and pass up the northern shoulder of the hill near the old Castle of Dunagore. "The general facts as to the two formations (the limestone and the coal measures here in contact) are few and simple. The limestone beds of the northern parts dip almost invariably south at a very gentle angle, not exceeding 1.30 on an average. A few local undulations occur in the beds. The general dip is south-south-west, and occasionally at angles as much as 10°. The limestone occasionally becomes buried deeper and deeper in that direction, under an increasing thickness of coal measures, amounting to 3,500 feet. The action of the sea upon the high coal-measure land may be observed both at Hag's Head and the cliffs of Moher, the waves eating away the lower part of the cliff, and constantly causing fragments of the upper part to fall for want of support. This action is considerably assisted by the great vertical joints, which traversing the rocks divide it into blocks, rendering the work of destruction a far easier matter than it would otherwise be.

"The best instance of this is at Ailleenasharragh at the cliffs of Moher. A steep and winding pathway leads the explorer (who should never stand alone or allow his companions to leave him alone) to the foot of this magnificent cliff; and the most casual observer cannot fail of being struck by the immense accumulation of debris which forms a talus on the beach, huge masses of grit shale and flag-stone lying piled together in wild confusion. Here the cliffs are constantly decreasing in altitude, inasmuch as the ground slopes inland from the coast, wherever on the other hand the slope of the surface is seaward, the height of the cliff is increasing."

As to accommodation for visitors and their comfort and safety, it must be remembered that the flag-fences, the series of steps, the round tables, the tower, the coach-house, &c., have been erected at the expense of the late C. O'Brien, Esq., M.P., who during his lifetime also employed servants to attend and cook for the visitors gratuitously.

Of this noble and lofty line of cliff "whose high unbending head looks fearfully in to the vasty deep," he would be a daring man who now-a-days would attempt a detailed verbal description.

But,-

> "Come on, Sir; here's the place:- stand still. -
>   How fearful
> And dizzy 'tis, to cast one's eye so low![1]
> The crows and choughs, that wing the midway air,
> Show scarce so gross as beetles: Halfway down
> Hangs one that gathers samphire; dreadful trade!
> Methinks he seems no bigger than his head:
> The fishermen that walk upon the beach,
> Appear like mice, and yon' tall anchoring bark,

---

[1] By trigonometrical survey Dover cliff is 313 feet high, or less than half the height of Moher.

> Diminish'd to her cock; her cock, a buoy
> Almost too small for sight: the murmuring surge,
> That on the unnumber'd idle pebbles chafes,
> Cannot be heard so high:- I'll look no more;
> Lest my brain turn, and the deficient sight
> Topple down headlong."

How curious that this sublime Shaksperian description so universally admired should have failed to please Dr. Samuel Johnson, who preferred a tame description of a temple by Congreve, saying with his usual rugged emphasis, "No, sir, it should be all precipice, all vacuum. The crows impede your fall. The impression is divided. You are not impressed with the horrible idea of immense height." And yet, as a matter of fact, no part of Moher Cliff does impress with the idea of immense height, more forcibly than just there where the little Island on which the two goats used to live, serves as a point of "computation," and shews the vast stages of the dreadful descent. "Samphire" is still collected and sold in Lahinch. But another "dreadful trade" is carried on over these cliffs for the capture of young sea birds, to make sale of their soft downy plumage.[1] The hardy cliffman descends some time in the month of June, having a rope round him, and hangs mid air rocking himself to and fro to reach the ledges on which the young birds sit secure, he lifts off his simple prey with a noose and secures them by the head under his belt or in a basket.

---

[1] Now illegal, and not carried on.

The elevation of Moher gives scope for the enjoyment of a grand panoramic view. On a clear day one sees the mountains of Killarney with Mangerton's grey head and sturdy form. The Galtees stand sentinels over south Tipperary, while Keeper guards it on the east. On the north the Needles or Nine Pins rear aloft their sharp pointed heads in serried array. And westwards to the sea extend the long low Isles of Arran. Moher is seen to best advantage by the active and nimble who walk all along the head of the cliff from the north. Then after exploring the Hag's Head and listening to tales of a submerged Church in Liscannor Bay they may enter the carriages ordered to meet them, and after a cooling draught from St. Bridget's Well, drive homeward highly exhilirated and thoroughly ozonized and satisfied, it is hoped, with glorious marine scenery.

But if the first visit is made on a bright and calm day, and the beauties and sublimity of the scene powerfully present themselves, visit Moher again and stay on while the setting sun illuminates with dazzling splendour cliff and headland, and tower and island, and then sinks in a halo of glory on the western horizon. And, friend, be persuaded to wait even longer still, yes, wait on until you have seen in what weird light the full moon hath touched with her silvery beams every prominent line of these lofty cliffs, while all the rest retire in awful gloom or grow up out of the night cloud.

But although a lame fiddler fell over the cliff in a fearful squall (it happened after dinner and we give the warning kindly) the best day to please our taste after many a visit to Moher is a day of gathering showers, advancing every half-hour or so in purple rage from the west, and of flying shadows of the driving clouds, and of screaming sea-birds, like thistle-down, wheeling on the wing, and of thundering surf, thundering more than ever as it tosses about the vast debris of fallen or falling rock in giant play, and the cliff trembles with the shock. And when one peeping over the edge may chance to espy a sailing vessel running for Galway or the Shannon; see how proudly she rises on the swell with her canvas lighted up in some stray sunbeam, and the waves that burst over her bows blaze out into a series of rainbows. The airy foam-beads are rushing across our eyes like a shower of rockets, and whirl high over head in scattering troops far away inland. In these things some feel a sense of rare delight, blended with awe indescribable.

SECOND EXCURSION.

Having admired the works of nature in their grand proportions as seen at the cliffs of Moher, it may be well to examine by way of contrast some works of human art, which stand in attestation of the laborious and not unscientific efforts which Ireland's earlier inhabitants made to secure themselves and their chattels from hostile invasion, also for purposes of religious worship.

Accordingly we may drive by the Ballyvaughan road, until we come to the Tuovaharan Chapel. This is a very simple structure on the road-side, and now dismantled, and is perhaps the oldest of the post-reformation structures of the kind in the County Clare. A curiously sculptured crucifixion is here exposed in a stone inserted in the walls, looking as made in the infancy or untutored period of art. The inscription runs thus:-

> "Pray for me, Mort. Hugh Flanagan,
> Priest of this Parish,
> Who built this altar in the year 1700."

The simple altar stands still in its place.

KILMOON.

Inside to the left of the Crag is the old Church of Kilmoon, and somewhat to the north in the valley the Church of Killeany, or of Eidne of Arran. This is not the original church, but one five centuries old in good preservation, - choir and nave 25 feet by 31 feet. The choir arch is a fine one in good preservation. Near are also some Cromlechs or Tombs over heroes slain in battle.

A CAHIR AGAIN.

Passing through a wild craggy district we now come to a Cahir or stone circular building, called Knick-knock-theen; this is of considerable dimensions, has an entrance with sloping jambs and flat single stone lintel. The gateway is still in excellent preservation. Passing for the present the church of Nouhaval, we now visit the very remarkable *Cahir of Ballykinvaraha*; this is seen from the road, and stands in a position well chosen for defence - it is of considerable extent. The door is to the south. If there were ever buildings inside they are not to be distinguished now, nor are their ruins traceable; but what makes this Cahir most remarkable is the external defence placed all round it. This consists of stones set on end for a space of some fifty yards all round the structure, evidently to obstruct an approaching enemy and break his order of battle. The same arrangement is remarked upon by Lord Dunraven as occurring in a Cahir on the Isles of Arran, (p. 6, Notes).

Another Cahir elsewhere may now be noticed. This is placed at the bottom of the Corkscrew hill, and has a fosse dug all round it. It is also remarkable for a doorway with a guard or watch house over it. There are other Cahirs at intervals along the entire intermediate way, up through the sloping ascent from the sea shore *(see Ordnance and Geological Maps)*, giving the idea of their having been constructed by those who were endeavouring to make good their way inland and establish themselves as they advanced. The same curious kind of structure is to be found in the Isles of Arran, in west Connaught and in Kerry, all being along the western main, and at points of easy access for a great band of emigrants driven to embark and to seek their homes "Westward, ho." Lord Dunraven in the volume we have alluded to, has associated the movement with the Firbolgs of traditionary lore; and from the fact of cells or oratories of the beehive form having been found in Gallarus, in Kerry, also of Dr. O'Donovan having found several such "built against the wall," has maintained that these structures were connected with the early monastic development of Christianity; others maintain that these were "Pagan fortresses," and nothing but places to keep cattle safe at night. Perhaps those without the Cloghauns are pagan, those within them are Christian. But as this question will not be settled in a hurry, it may be well to turn back a short way, and to pay a visit to a class of structure undeniably ancient and Christian.

OF NOUHAVAL.

Approaching the old Church we find a kind of Pillar Stone or Market Cross seeming to have indicated the spot as a centre of attraction. A curious old cross much eaten away by weather calls attention. The Church has a chancel, and is divided from the nave by a fine stone arch, which marks its date. The stones are even in size, well hammered, and nicely adjusted to each other; but at the rere of the church is an oratory which the natives call the tomb of the O'Davorans. The dimensions of this are 25 feet 6 inches by 18 feet 3 inches, and at top of gable 18 feet 9 inches to surface level. The south wall is much decayed, but traces undoubtedly remain of the structure having had its interior spanned by a barrel vault, helping to support the stone roof which ran up outside into a sharp angle above, very much like St. Kevin's oratory and others of the period.

Kilfenora is now reached, and we enter the Cathedral of St. Fachnan by a simple arched doorway over which a bishop's head is inserted in the wall and stands out in bold relief. As to the name Kilfenora some say it comes from Kil, a church, and Fanore, an elevated and fertile place. Indeed there is such a name and place occurring on the sea road from Arran View to Black Head. Ware, evidently quiet astray, says honestly: "There are no accounts that I know of to be depended upon concerning the time of the foundation of the episcopal see of Fenabore, or who was the first bishop of it." The attempt at a tower is conspicuously mean and hideous. A pile of emigrants' luggage with a rabbit-hutch or bird-cage overhead would look equally imposing. The breadth of the church is 20 feet 10 inches, and the walls are 3 feet thick. The window in the east gable is semicircular, 14 feet 7 inches, and about 20 feet high, divided into three compartments by two triangular-based pillars, each compartment circular-headed, and the whole line with finely-chiselled stones on the inside. The middle division is 1 foot 4 inches, and each of the outside ones is eleven inches wide. The effect is very striking. This part of the structure was covered by a fine old oak roof within the present century, but it was allowed to be stripped and made a ruin of. In the north-east corner of the Church is a niche in the side wall formed by two pointed small arches sustained in the middle by a slender column of a stone. In front of this niche is a tombstone level with the ground, shewing the figure of an ecclesiastic with folded arms across the chest. There is another niche in the north wall, nearly opposite, in the same style, surmounted by a head and mitre, in front of which, and level with the ground, is a tombstone having an ecclesiastic in full costume, with a chalice in his hand. There is an inscription to Hygate Lone, or *Love* as some will have it:-

> "Here lyeth the body of Hygate Lone,
> Who lived 21 years Dean of this Church, and died
> in September, 1638."

There are lengthy inscriptions in Latin to the R.C. bishop, Neylan, also to Donaldus M'Donogh and his wife Maria O'Conor. A sad inscription records the early deaths of several children of Dean Neptune Blood, the second of that name. From a translation in the hands of some members of the family the following is taken:-

> " 'Man goeth forth as a flower and vanishes
> like a shadow.'
> "Thus silently have fled those dear pledges
> of their parents' love. Should you desire to
> know their names, and when they died, behold,
> subscribed are characters which explain all to
> you. Neptune, son of Rev. Neptune, and of
> his wife Isabella Blood, alias Pullein, died on
> the 1st of July, 1683, the 13th month," &c.

And so on through seven little children, including

> "The amiable Deborah, the godly and truly
> fine youth William, and the facetious Neptune."

There is outside, near the south wall of chancel, a Latin inscription over a Mr. Lysaght in which he gets very great credit indeed for having lived a peaceable, pure and sober life in the last century.

A chapel projects from the north-east angle measuring 28 feet 3 inches by 18 feet 10 inches. Near the window is a stone cross lying about, with a figure of a bishop in canonicals engraven on it holding a crozier or bachal.

A very fine cross stands in a field to the west, sculptured on all sides, and having a rude representation of a crucifixion on the east side. This cross is about 15 feet high, 3 feet wide at bottom, 2 feet 6 inches at 6 feet from the ground, and 10 inches thick, but tapering somewhat to the arms upwards.

There were three such other crosses at the cardinal points from the church; two fell down or were broken, one is in Clarisford, Killaloe. These are supposed to have been marks of the Termon, or church-lands.

A well with a covering and inscription is worth a visit, erected by one of the MacDonogh family. Other ruins, as Castle na Wogga, or the Castle of Ridicule, are near at hand, and in a stream near Fanta are fossil remains.

THE THIRD EXCURSION.

The third excursion may be to Ennistymon and the villages of Lahinch and Liscannor.

Passing down by

KILSHANNY

one may desire to learn that in this humble valley
were born Hugh and Andrew M'Curtin before the
last century began its course. Hugh was a poet and
made his way to high distinction in Paris, but first
suffered imprisonment in Newgate for some literary
production not acceptable to the Government.[1] He
made his way in Paris, becoming tutor to some
distinguished individual - the Dauphin, if we
recollect aright - in 1732, and writing his English-
Irish Dictionary, dedicated "Illustrissimo D. D.
Abbati de Vaubrun, Doctori Socio Sorbonico,
Collegii Hibernorum Parisiis Superiori." In the
preface he pronounces thus of the Irish: "Of all the
dead and the living languages none is more copious
and elegant in expression, nor is any more
harmonious and musical in pronunciation."
Another Kilshanny man has also distinguished
himself in literature, Mr. Thynne, author of Logic,
and an edition of Livy.

The glens of

ENNISTYMON

are a sweet retreat on a broiling summer's day. The
overshadowing trees affording a grateful shade, and
the babbling brook a grateful music. The glens open
out into the Ennistymon River, and the pleasure-
grounds and garden of Ennistymon House,

---

[1] "A Discourse in Vindication of the Antiquities of Ireland."

heretofore kindly open under due restrictions, give a pleasant space for a stroll until one comes in view of the grand cascade of the River Cullenagh tumbling down, after a flood, its tawny waters with a grand roaring. The house was enlarged, and in fact grafted on a castle, by Major C. O'Brien who afterwards sold the estate to Judge Finucane, from whom it has come into the hands of the ancient family of the M'Namaras of Doolin.

Although trees are so scarce about Ennistymon it is related in the Parochial Survey that an old man named Michael Daly, who died about the beginning of the century at a very advanced age, asserted that almost the entire country about Ennistymon was, within his recollection, covered with woods, mostly oak and ash, full grown, and that he frequently shot wild pheasants in those woods. He was Mr. O'Brien's huntsman.

Passing by a conventual establishment, recently erected in a prominent position overlooking Ennistymon, and leaving the Union Workhouse to the left, one reaches the curious old town of Lahinch or Lahensy, the name indicating that the place was "Half an Island."

Should the order of the day be to visit the Glens of

MOY

or Glenville, we turn south, and near Sir A. Fitzgerald's handsome marine residence, stroll through these pleasant glens with many a sweet orchidaceous plant in flower, and many a bright and sometimes rare butterfly floating in the sunny air.

Near this were the pits sunk for coal, but abandoned. Here, and generally speaking throughout west Clare, an entomologist may find abundant scope for work; insect life of certain kinds abounds, although it is only the most attractive group, the *Lepidoptera*, that has been at all exhaustively studied. All along the west coast the beautiful butterfly *Colias Edusa*, the Clouded Yellow, crosses our path in summer, though not in great profusion. The group most abundant and conspicuous is the splendid family of the Vanessas. Walls may be seen at times almost entirely covered with painted ladies and red admirals; and fields

> "Where the brilliant peacock, Io,
> Loves to spread his painted pinions,
> Loves to sip the liquid honey."

In some places may be seen, and in certain years in marvellous profusion, a small strange-looking moth, with velvety black body and clear red wings flying languidly in the sunshine, as if blind, for a few weeks in June. This is the very rare "Burnet" moth *Zygaena Minos* so seldom met with in any other part of the United Kingdom. From the occurrence of this and certain other entomological "rarities" occurring also in the western parts of the Spanish peninsula, a distinguished English entomologist has drawn a curious and elaborate argument in proof of the theory that a connexion by land must have existed in former ages between the west coast of these two countries; for the details of which however we must refer the reader to "the books."

But should it be desired to visit Liscannor, the road runs down through the sandhills and passes the now dismantled

This castle, together with that of Ballinalacken, were specially exempted from the destruction which befel so many other castles in Clare under Cromwell's regime.   D. O'Brien presented a petition as an innocent person, and having proved this to the satisfaction of the Commissioners sitting at Loughrea, the following order was issued by Colonel Stubber, which is copied from the original now before us.

"Loughrea, 13th Sept., 1654.

"Upon consideration hadd of this Petition, Quartermaster Smith, on service for demolishinge of castles in the Countie of Clare, is hereby required to forbear demolishinge the within mentioned - pass of Dough, and the within mentioned ruinous Castell of Ballinalackin until further order, and until the Lord President, and the rest that are joined with him, do send further order at our next meeting, in regard they are now absent herefrom, you are not to faile. And for soe doing, this shall be your authority. In Quartermaster Smith's absence, any other employed as aforesaid is to observe this order.

"G. V. STUBBER.

"Date ut supra."

The village of

is called after the O'Connors who once held large tracts of this county, but parted with them chiefly to the O'Briens in rather a hurry, on the eve of some change in Queen Elizabeth's time. The village is mainly indebted for its harbour, such as it is, to Mr. Cornelius O'Brien, who got a grant, and was aided by others. The neighbouring clergy and gentry provided large assistance in money, food and work for the people starving during the terrible famine of 1822. The mackerel fishery is carried on in Liscannor bay with some vigour during the season by about twenty boats or corraghs. The sprat rise occasionally in great broad quivering patches on the surface, and innumerable sea birds gather overhead screaming and pouncing on their prey, and the young sharks sail round and round in swift graceful curves, and occasionally a bottlenose whale comes the way spouting a jet of water about him, and all the while the fisherman is pulling in the round glittering snapping fish as fast as he can work his weary arms. Such a lively hour as this is not every day to be enjoyed; but it is well worth trying the luck of an ordinary common mackerel day, and the boatmen are very civil and obliging to sporting ladies and gentlemen, who honour them with their patronage and silver. This is a good place also for a turbot, which those fonder of fish than of fishing may readily secure; indeed the people of the entire district are remarkably intelligent, and wonderfully versed in the old stories and lore of their localities.

We omit the story of this Church under the waves and of the earthquake (of Lisbon) and no end of ship-wrecks, apparitions to seamen, speaking mermaids and the like. The people also will talk about smugglers and smuggling, now a thing of the distant past; but poor old Paddy Connors is dead, a repertory of such lore - indeed, the late Mr. Eugene O'Curry pronounced the people of these regions "a thousand degrees more historically intelligent than the Lagenians or Ossorian's;" and he or some other authority mentions how a process server lately living in Ardrahan was the direct representative of a king of Connaught; and many others there are occupying but humble positions due to changes of the wheel of fortune and to the ups and downs and merry-go-round transfers of property and position in the west of Ireland, who now have to work slowly upward once again by energy, ability and self-command.

THE FOURTH EXCURSION.

Turning eastward by O'Donovan's house, the parish of

KILCORNEY

is soon reached. Kilcorney Church is in ruins, and all gone except the south wall. There is a holy well in the same valley dedicated to Inghean Bhaoith, the daughter of Boetius, and a princess of the Dalcasian race, who had to do with Kilenaboy Church. The Caves of Kilcorney are remarkable, they are situated in a beautiful little valley, and are good instances of subterraneous channels in limestone. One of them can be explored to a considerable distance; after heavy rain it discharges great floods over the adjacent fields, and in the course of time has produced a fine alluvial deposit. The peasantry have a legend that after a very heavy flood a herd of wild horses issued from the cave and overran the country; there is also another legend of the water being enchanted and performing some surprising actions. A few lines may be here inserted bearing on these subjects, the effusion of a native child of song, an humble Irish school-master:-

> "The thirsting swain who happened then
> To raise the cup found nothing in;
> And the poor crone, intent to bake
> With restless hands the morning cake,
> Sudden beheld it crumbling pour
> Upon the fire in formless flour.
> The faithless drops that held it on
> The bars consolidate, were gone.
>
> . . . .
>
> Now, from the sombre mouth appearing,
> Come wheeling on as goodly fair
> A troop of steeds as ever were,
> Speeding over earthly plain
> With flowing tail and dancing mane,
> Riderless and reinless straying
> With heads on high and joyous neighing,
> Onward they come with equal speed,
> Still seeking where they used to feed,
> Nor slacken pace until the leader
>
> . . . .

Back, back they shy, they wheel around,
The watchers from their ambush bound,
Make at the herd - 'twas all in vain.
Back to the cave again they sped,
Again it thundered to their tread.
The uproar, through the cavern's breast,
Rolled, lessening till it sunk to rest;
But having caught one weakly filly
Of the wild herd, unschooled and silly,
Betimes she grew till such a mare
For bulk of limb and power to bear
Ne'er Burren saw, since or before:
Where many a goodly foal she bore,
And where even yet her breed is shewn
Pre-eminent for strength and bone."

But as to the simple facts about the inside of the cave. In Gough's Camden the following description is given:-

"The mouth is level with the plain, and is three feet in diameter; then the passage is blocked up and widens: forty yards from floor is a deep pit seven or eight yards over, after which the floor is even for 20 yards. Dr. Charles Lucas never passed beyond the pit." This gentleman was a native of Corofin, and the son of Benjamin Lucas, of Ballinagaddy, and of Miss Blood, daughter of Dean Blood. This Benjamin was son of Col. Benjamin Lucas who, with his brothers, Captain Thomas and Lieutenant Samuel, came over with Cromwell. Dr. C. Lucas was born in 1713; graduated in T.C.D.; was an M.D.; also of R.C.S. London; and took an active part in the stirring contests which agitated Dublin and the corporations. [1] He was also M.P. with Mr. Latouche for Dublin City. Dr. Samuel Johnson was captivated by his conversational powers and varied information, and expressed surprise at the hostility he encountered.

It may be remarked here that it was Dr. C. Lucas who first discovered the iron spa at Lisdoonvarna.

Leaving Rockview on the left, the road comes out on the Lemaneagh and Ballyvaughan line, and following it a short space one finds a bye way leading to Termon Cottage and Templecronan Church.

TEMPLE CRONAN.

This is a small Church in beautiful preservation, and "nearly as old as Christianity in Ireland." Mr. J. O'Donovan asserts it is called after Cronan, who was doubtless the same better known in connection with a great religious house at Roscrea, or Tomgraney rather as Dr. Lanigan relates - It is a small Ermidhe or Oratory, measuring in length on the inside 21 feet, and in breadth 12 feet 9 inches. The south wall, which is built of large stones, is featureless; but the north wall contains a pointed doorway, which is obviously of a date much later than the original structure itself. The west gable contains a semi-Cyclopean doorway, in height from present level, 5 feet 6 inches, and in breadth 1 foot

---

[1] Rutty, who hated him and never let a line of Lucas' able scientific speculations on Spas into the "Dublin Philosophical Society's Transactions," called him "Apothecary."

11 inches at top, and 2 feet 5 inches at bottom. The lintel which traverses this doorway at top is 5 feet long and 7 inches high. The modern doorway (which was broken at the north wall when the doorway in east gable was built up) is 5 feet 5 inches in height from the present ground-level, and 3 feet 4 inches in width from spring of the arch. The east gable contains a window which presents all the features of primeval times. It is quadrangular on the inside, and perfectly round-headed on the outside. It measures, on inside 4 feet 7 inches in height, and in breadth at top, 1 foot 8½ inches, and at bottom, 2 feet 5 inches. The side walls are 8 feet high.

The following additional items are given in Lord Dunraven's sumptuously illustrated volume which has two photographs of this church, and detailed engravings of its several specialities. The ruin is beautifully placed in the midst of a grove of noble old ash trees, some of great size, the stem of one measuring 21 feet in circumference. This grove of trees, and the still more venerable ruin overshadowed by them, stand in the centre of a picturesque dell, bounded by a limestone scarp which rises in a perpendicular line at one side of the Church to a height of 20 feet.

The Church is about the oldest looking and most interesting I have seen in this part of Ireland. The masonry is very antient and massive in character. The stones in the south wall are of great size, one 6 feet long by 1 foot deep. In north wall the stones are not so large, and a little grouting the only cement used. The roof was high and steep; the quoins are hammered and rounded, and there were projecting stones at each corner. The two at the south corners are ornamented with scroll patterns cut in relief, while animals' heads in a row project from the cornice, and here and there on the face of the western wall strange human heads project in some instances, the faces more animal than human, the eyes sunken, and the lower part of the face projecting.

The doorway is square-headed with inclined sides, a carved head at each side. The east window is very remarkable. The pellet moulding may be seen running down the face of the southern jamb, and the stone itself does not look like an insertion. There are also mouldings on the quoins at the east end; but only three stones have this ornament. The whole character of this building is one of great antiquity; but how can we account for the appearance of the mouldings, the pellet, the head, and the angle, in company with such manifestly primitive work"? So far these authorities. It may be added that the height of the gables is 19 ft. 6 in., and not one stone is wanting in either of them. The five carved heads are on the outside of the south gable, as already mentioned. The altar is still standing. Out of the window grows the ash tree, without any earth to nourish or cover its roots. The floor of the church is quite level: no graves inside. There are numerous head and tombstones without a single inscription on any of them. This church seems to have been roofed with large flagstones, which are quite numerous, and now used to cover graves. The end walls are only single stones from the inner line to the top. In the churchyard are two cumdachs intended for bones (as Mr. J. O'Donovan pronounces them to be for), said to have been erected by St. Cronan; they are formed of large flagstones, so placed as to meet at the top like the roof of a church. Near the church is a well, called after Cronan. To the north-west are to be seen the pedestal and staff of a cross of considerable height, and it is said there were others which marked the limits of the church land of Cronan.

CARRON AND SLADOO.

"In Carron parish are two other churches, viz., Carron and Sladoo. The latter is very remarkable in some respects. There is a small square window in the north wall, near the altar, which is standing; height 2 ft., width 1 ft. 6 in., and no east window. The altar is erected of five stories, height 5 ft., width 3 ft. 2 in. The gables project over the side walls 1 ft. 6 in. The south wall is propped by two supports. The walls are built of very small stones, the gables rounded at the corners. The roof seems to have been arched like a bridge. There is a bench all round the side of the walls, which was used as seats. There are no carved stones in or near the building. There is a remarkable comdach. An antiquary adds the pleasing information, that "This church seems to have been used as a schoolroom on week days, and on Sundays, before and after divine service, as a shebeen shop. There is a cross wall 4 ft. from the altar which separates the altar from view of the remainder of the house; the wall is three feet high. On the top may have been a wooden screen. The church is situated on the top of a bare hill; near hand are two circular cahirs - one near the east end, the other at the back of the church. These are not broken up or disturbed as in so many other cases."

GLEN COLUMKILLE.

Turning eastward, after leaving Termon, we enter the beautiful valley of Glen Columkille. Here is an old church dedicated to Saint Columkille, about five centuries old. The east gable and south wall only stand; most likely there was here an earlier oratory, as at Nouhaval, at Carran, and elsewhere. Here perhaps, the north wall of the old may have been grafted into the new structure, where it is dressed and bevelled. A highly ornamented tomb is here erected in memory of Captain Cornelius O'Brien, who was grandson to General Murtagh O'Brien, who was brother to Murrough, first Earl of Inchiquin; also, another plain one to the Mahon family.

GEOLOGY.

The hills on the east side of this valley form beautiful examples of the step-like succession of cliffs and bare rock. The beds here are generally horizontal.

THE EAGLE'S ROCK.

Near the north end of the valley, and forming the east side of Slieve Carran, is the magnificent cliff of

Kinallia, or the Eagle's Rock, sheer 500 feet in perpendicular height. The most striking view in Burren, and the one giving the best idea of a typical "mountain limestone" district, is that from the new road which winds up the steep hill westward from Columkill cottage. Beneath you lies Glen Columkille, its green fields and dark woods contrasting finely with the bare[1] rocky-terraced hills of grey limestone; while stretching away in the background may be seen the hills in the neighbourhood of Gort, of silurian and old red sandstone. Near this are some curious gorges, hollows, and "corries," as Glenulla, Clab, Poulavellan, and Voula laughan. At Glencullen, a small copper vein was unsuccessfully worked some years ago. At the foot of the Eagle's Nest are situated

THE HERMITAGE OF ST. M'DUAGH AND THE CELEBRATED BOHERNAMIAS.

His little oratory the saint constructed in a dismal spot of a gloomy valley, haunted by wolves and stricken with famine. The structure, though much dilapidated, is easily recognized to have been intended for a church. It was very small, and only one gable and one side wall remain. The gable faces the cliff and is featureless. The side wall contains a small rude quadrangular window, 10ft. by 5in.

---

[1] This and other peculiarities of the Burren limestone field have been treated of with great ability by Dr. S. Westropp, in a paper read before the Geological Society of Ireland.

outside to the east. This is certainly the original oratory of Mac Duagh, in which the great king of Connaught discovered the saint, and induced him to remove to Kilmacduagh, where he built a sumptuous monastery for him, and where a round tower and other strange antique structures will reward the artist, antiquary, and tourist who may visit them. Immediately to the east of Temple Macduagh, is Tober-macduagh, and over this little church to the north-west is a cave, called Mac Duagh's bed, in which the saint slept, and about twenty perches off is shown the grave of his servant, who did not survive the substantial meal he took off the flying dishes after his having been emaciated from long use of herbs in the wilderness. On Easter day, it seems the king was feasting, and the saint and his servant were fasting, whereupon the servant or clerk, not able to stand the acute pangs of hunger any longer, directed the saint's attention to the king's good dinner, and requested him to try the power of prayer in hopes of a share.

> "Pray, oh, pray, and let the sinner
> For the saint forego his dinner."

Accordingly, just as

> "The royal host o'er bullock bends,
> Grasps skene, looks round him, and cries, Friends,
> I await your orders. Who says beef?'"

Even then the hungry saint had

> "Breathed his prayer on heaven's ear;
> Oh! if thou lovest me, send it here."

Even then his prayer was granted. The rout and the orderly flight of the dishes are then described, also the rage and pursuit of the king and his hungry guests.

> 'Ah!' cried Gorra, as he drove
> Up-hill, and saw the work above;
> Saw his own fair banquet strown
> Further on o'er sward and stone,
> With hungry saint and servant squatted
> Down beside, and working at it.
> 'Aha! my lads, I have you there.'

> "'Saint,' roared the clerk - *another prayer*-
> Knife and cup to earth were thrown,
> Down went Duach on marrow bone;
> 'Oh! if thy servant grace has found,
> Chain them yonder to the ground.'
> And lo, both king and retinue
> Are fastened to the flags in view.

> "Sceptic, dost thou doubt my tale
> Then, see where truth has set its seal,
> Where the dish has signed the flag;
> Where the wine has stained the crag,
> You behold the legend proved
> In the granite pawed and hoov'd."

(From Village Musings by E. Burke.)

Mr. Foote attributes the marks to the effect of rain, not prayer; but this is too prosaic for Paddy.

The new quay and Ballyvaughan line of road brings the party to a point near

In Lord Dunraven's work, the meaning of the word is explained as pointing at the situation of those churches, "On the breast of the high pass." His lordship recommends a visit to be paid "in the earliest hour of morning, to enjoy the full poetry and charm of the scene. In the early morn, the women, bearing their milk-pails on their heads, may be seen ascending the mountains with free elastic step, and their voices heard across the hills as they call their cows to their side for milking. The red and purple dresses of these women, the cattle, the rich green pasture form strong and delightful contrasts of colours to the grey tones of the scene; and the faint odour of fresh milk from the pails, borne on the clear pure air of morning, the silence only broken, by the ringing laughter of the women, as they meet in groups and chat gaily before commencing their homeward path. All combine to form a scene of fresh and healthy life, the beauty of which is only strengthened when the sun breaking forth from amid the clouds casts in long rays a veil of delicate silvery light over the steep mountain side." A detailed description is superfluous; the large stones of cyclopean construction, sloping jambs, square-headed doors, &c., indicating the age of these remarkable structures. The drive home by the Corkscrew Hill at sunset is very fine.

THE FIFTH EXCURSION

The drive now to be taken is a long one, and the start must be early. Passing down by Ballinalacken

Castle, the preservation of which from ruin has been noted, we now journey forward, with the sea on one side in all its varied aspects of colour, and with its ceaseless vibrations, sometimes in the "low and sweet voice" of nature's music; sometimes in tones of thunder, but as ever sounding in the minor key; and on the other hand are rocks - rocks in hills and vales, in slopes and curves, in articulations of strength and endurance, as though one had in veritable view the backbone of Ireland, as a little boy, cleverly enough, called the stupendous formation. One passes along this road with a sea of waters just underneath on the one side, in what mood soever the sea may choose to be, and with a sea of rocks on the other, stereotyped in that tossed and tortured variety of elevation and depression which igneous agency may have wrought, or else smoothed and polished in the cliffs over Glanina by grounding icebergs and slipping glaciers, or else eaten into and fissured, as rain or tides may have found spots of weaker texture to give way. And so one passes along, mile after mile, up to Black Head; the coast-line presenting varying aspects at every turn, and rugged grandeur of every degree. And here, too, the lover of botany may linger and stoop into these fissures to find Alpine plants, of which old Mackay wrote, and others more recently.

BURREN

From a formal treatise "On the Distribution of Plants in Burren," by the late F.J. Foot, Esq., the following may be taken for the information of strangers who may desire to cultivate in new forms the accomplishment of botany: - Burren possesses a Flora, probably the most remarkable, for the extent of the district, in the United Kingdom. Many rare plants grow here in abundance, often in abnormal situations, and almost all in the limestone among the chinks and crevices. The plants are divided into four groups:

1st, Those abundantly and rather equally divided over the whole district.

2nd, Those confined to a portion of the district, and abundantly distributed throughout that portion.

3rd, Those growing locally, but in colonies.

4th, Those occurring locally.

These lists are exclusive of the grasses, carices, mosses, and lichens.

The characteristic, or otherwise remarkable plants are now given, with the number of the group, to which it belongs, also the locality.

GROUP FIRST

No. 4. Arabis Hirsuta; abundant.
8. Arenaria Verna; ditto.
9. Cerastium Arvense; everywhere, most beautiful and typical.
11. Geranium Sanguineum; everywhere among rocks.
12. Euonymus Europœus; everywhere among rocks.
20. Geum Rivale; in most extraordinary places.

24. Rubus Saxatilis; equally abundant.
30. Agrimonia Eupatoria; abundant everywhere.
32. Sedum Acre; highly characteristic; everywhere.
33. Saxifraga Hypnoides; everywhere; and covers ant-hills.
35. Sanicula Europöea, everywhere, in all situations.
38. Rubia Peregrina, the dyer's madder; in abundance everywhere in Burren.
41. Galium Pusillum; everywhere; very abundant in spring and summer in rocks.
44. Asperula Cynanchica; all over Burren.
45. Valeriana Officinalis; very characteristic and common.
46. Valeriana Rubra.
48. Gnaphalium Dioicum, not abundant.
59. Chlora Perfoliata; not abundant everywhere.
76. Juniperus Nana; typical Burren plant.
77. Taxus Baccata; on steep cliffs.
78. Triglochin Palustre; high ground in moisture.
81. Listera Ovata; everywhere abundant.
85. Orchis Pyramidalis; everywhere.
87. Gymnadenia Conopsea; fragrant like hyacinth.
94. Polystichum Aculeatum; in chinks.
95. _____ Lobatum; abundant.
102. Asplenium Ruta Muraria; luxuriant, large.
103. _____ Trichomanes.

106. Scolopendrium Vulgare; "Burren, the home of heartstongue."

GROUP SECOND.

1. Thalictrum Majus; abundant on hill side, south of Black Head.
2. _____ Minus.
6. Helianthemum Canum; rare and beautiful, north of Poulsallagh, in Ballyran.
17. Spiraea Filipendula; in Glen Columkille and Eagle's Rock, supposed of medicinal value for kidney disease.
18. Drysas Octopetala; "like a carpet." Sedum Rhodiola.
50. Arbutus Uva Ursi; on hill west of Ballyvaughan, its habitat illustrates connection of botany and geology.
51. Pyrola Media; west of Ballyvaughan, south of Ballyalleban, or Slevecarran.
56. Gentiana Verna; abundant, beautiful, typical.
63. Orobanche Rubra; parasitical, as thymus; Ballyvaughan hills.
80. Epipactis Ovalis; Orchid, hills Ballyvaughan; emits a tinkling sound.
91. Habenaria Viridis; Ballyvaughan, Slievecarran, Clab.
104. Asplenium Marinum; near Ballyvaughan.
111. Cystopteris Fragilis; ends abruptly at Coalmeasures.

112.   Osmunda Regalis; not in limestone, but in
       shady ravines in Lisdoonvarna, Moher,
       and Lehinch.

110.   Adiantum Capillus Veneris; "The
       Maiden's Hair Fern;" the most elegant of
       our native ferns; near Blackhead and
       Ballyryan, Poulsallagh, Ballyvaughan
       valley, on both sides, in open joints and
       faces of cliffs; sometimes very rich.

GROUP FOURTH.

13.   Rhamnus Catharticus; handsome rare
       shrub; near Ballyvaughan, in low
       grounds.
       Potentilla Comarum.
       Sedum telephium.
36.   Sambucus Ebulus; dwarf-elder; crags near
       Ballyvaughan.
42.   Galium Boreale; Ballyvaughan,
       Ballyalliban.
72.   Ajuga Pyramidalis; rare; near Poulsallagh,
       in a small area near coast road.
73.   Statice Spatulata; not far from last plant, on
       low cliffs by roadside.
76.   Orchis Pyramidalis; a truly typical Burren
       plant.
       ___ Var Floriplena.
89.   Habenaria Albida; pretty; on
       Coalmeasures, near Lisdoonvarna.

92. Ophrys Apifera; decidedly rare; on but one spot near Acres' village, Ballyvaughan.

113. Botrychium Lunaria; occurs at several places.

The most remarkable of Burren plants appear to be found along the sea road, at Ballysallagh, on the heights over Black Head, and in Ballyvaughan valley.

In the course of the present excursion, those to whom very old churches are ever a novelty and matter of interest, may find two most curious specimens of this class in the parish of

KILLONAGHAN

The original church is said to have been erected by St. Columbkille, after his expulsion from Arran by St. Einne (Tantæ ne iræ cœlestibus animis?).[1] This is

---

[1] The following are some lines of the Saint's Lament, as translated by T. O'Flanagan, in "Transactions of Gaelic Society":-

"Farewell from me to Aran,
    A sad farewell to my feeling;
    I am eastward to Hy,
    And it is separated since the flood.

"Farewell from me to Aran,
    It is this anguishes my heart,
    Not to be westward at her waves
    Amidst groups of the saints of heaven.

"Though there should be no existing life,
    But hearing of the angels of Aran;
    Better than any life under heaven
    To hear their hymns of praise."

in the townland of Graggagh. Two gables in tolerable preservation, 48 feet by 21 feet, walls of large stones, not laid in regular courses, and 2 ft. 3 in. in thickness. Window in east is perfect.

But in the townland of *Crumlin*, are ruins of another church of even greater antiquity, and probably this was the original church built by St. Columkille. The walls are built of large stones, not laid in regular courses, but well grouted with strong mortar. The east window may have been of subsequent insertion; but all the rest looks very antient, and undoubtedly belongs to the primitive ages of Christianity in Ireland. And here, one cannot but remark how strange it seems to find names of founders of churches, with other traces, more or less decisive connected with graves, and wells and annual celebrations far away in these wild marine regions. And yet, one finds these names again in what may be reverently termed full-blown ecclesiastical dignity and splendour, scattered far inland, and associated with positions of the highest importance and eminence. Thus, to mention a few: St. Flannan is noted by O'Flaherty as connected with a little maritime parish in West Connaught, and afterwards emerges bishop of Killaloe; St. Camins church we visited in Carran parish; but he reappears in Tomgraney, say some; in Roscea say others. So, too, Duach left the hungry valley and the shadow of the Eagle's Nest. For Columkille's exploits and wanderings, one must refer to the historians. And St. Brendan's voyages seem to have outdone those of the most adventurous of sea-traversing missionaries. St. Kevin's brother has his name associated with Nouhaval.

But now we have rounded Black Head, and are running along the south shore of the Bay of Galway, through Glanina, and pass the precious roadside well Tobercornan and into Ballyvaughan, now supplied besides with water "by the enlightened munificence" of Lord Annally through his agent, Mr. W. Lane Joynt. The most attractive object in this neighbourhood (always allowing as an exception the mollusks of the Redbank), is the ancient

ABBEY OF CORCOMROE.

This is situate in the parish of Abbey; and of it Archdall, in "Monasticon" gives the following account:- "A.D., 1194 - Donald, King of Limerick, founded a sumptuous monastery here for Cistertian

monks, and dedicated it to the Virgin Mary; others say that Donagh Carbrac, his son was the founder, anno 1200. This Abbey was also called the Valley of the Fruitful Rock, and was a daughter of that of Suire. It was afterwards made subject to the celebrated Abbey of Furnes in Lancashire.

"A.D., 1267 - D. O'Brien, King of Thomond, was killed in the battle that was fought at Suidane (in the barony of Burren). He was solemnly interred in this Abbey, where a grand monument was erected to his memory, the remains of which are to be seen to this day.

"A.D., 1317 - A dreadful battle was fought near this town, in which many of the principal of the O'Briens fell; amongst the slain were Teige and Murtagh Garbh, sons of Brian Ruadh, King of Thomond", so far Archdall.

As to the connexion of Corcomroe with the Abbey of Furnes, the following is taken from "Becks's Annales Furnesienses 1844":- "In 1249, the Abbot of Clairvaux, with the consent of General Chapter, placed four monasteries under the control of Furnes Abbey, to be unto her as daughters. These were De Castro Dei, De Sancta Cruce, De Petra Fertili, and De Suris, according to their monastic title . . . . De Petra Fertili, or Corcomroe, antiently Corcommath, in the County Clare, formed, in 1197, but according to other authorities in 1194, by Donald, King of Limerick, or by his son, Donagh Carbrac, in 1200, for Cistertian monks, was a daughter of the Abbey of Suire originally" (p. 213)

The following is the substance of the traditionary lore on the subject as given by the late J. O'Donovan:- "the Abbey was founded by the son of Conor-na-Suidane O'Brien on the spot where his father was killed in the battle by G. O'Shaughnessy, of Dungaire, near Kinvarra, and an effigy was placed on the spot where he fell." - *From the "Annals of Innisfallen."*

"An army was led by Conor-na-Suidane, the son of Donagh Carbreac O'Brien, to Kineh Fearmiac, they were joined by O'Dea and O'Hehir at the head of their forces. They went to the upper Canthred to bring the inhabitants here to submission, and they burned the country north of Duibh Gleaun, and proceeded north to Beal Cloghaidh, near the sea, where they were met by Conor O'Loughlin and his allies, and a battle ensued, in which Conor-na-Suidane O'Brien, and a great many of his people, were slain by O'Loghlin, and he Conor-na-Suidane, was buried by the monks "who raised a monument over his grave," adds another of the ancient authorities. This monument is still in existence in the choir of the Abbey called the

monument of "Crohoor-na-Suidane." It is very like
the tomb of Conan Gall O'Kane, or Cahan, in the
church of Dungiven, but in far better preservation. It
is unfortunately crowded out of sight by a tomb,
large indeed but rude, on which there is an
inscription in modern letters -

"The burial place of O'Loghlin
King of Burren."

But we must not omit the description of the Hag of
Ballyvaughan, who it seems had much to do with
the sanguinary proceedings which led to the
foundation of Corcomroe, "Magrath, the Homer of
Ireland, thus describes her as encountered at Lough
Raska, near Ballyvaughan."

"The heroes of Broadswords advanced silently in
close array, until they reached the banks of Lough
Rasqua. All the host viewed the bright lake together,
they beheld on its white margin a deformed sprite,
who struck them with amazement, it was a hag with
blue face, withered aspect, green teeth, rough hair,
sharp bent nails, her hair was fretted, rough, strong,
&c., of a grey reddish colour, her forehead narrow,
full of lumps, deeply furrowed in irregular ridges,
every hair of her eyebrows, which were of a reddish
grey colour was like unto a strong, tough fishing
hook. Her eyes, like red berries, with soft and scarlet
margins, were sharp-sighted, though flaming with
unearthly glare, and looking out between rough
bristled eye-lashes." We omit, as too dreadful for the
nineteenth century, details of her nose, also her
mouth, her bearded upper lip, and her two, long,

slender, sharp, black-coloured teeth. She had a cairn of heads before her, a load of weapons, a bundle of long bones, which she was washing in the lake, the waters of which were stained and soiled with refuse and floating with tangled hair.

A conference ensues between this amiable beauty and the heads of the army, who got her flung into the lake, out of which she ascended and uttered horrible maledictions. They marched on, however, met Terlagh O'Brien. The Dalcassians fought a great battle outside the Abbey, the site of which is still pointed out, and bones of the slain often turned up. The Hag goes still by the name Caileach Cuin Boirùè, or the Hag of Black Head. May we never encounter her by sea, by land or by lake.

THE SIXTH EXCURSION

must be short and easy for those who may not like long rides, even though the scenery be sublime and varied, and the objects interesting. So the road is taken towards the sea near

DOOLIN

same as Dublin or "the black pool." Near the road side are some of those "swallow holes" caused by the falling in of the roofs of subterranean caverns. These are mostly on the boundary line between the shales and the limestone, the upper surface giving way to the pressure of water. One also may look with strange wonder at the burying place of the Spaniards, near the entrance to St. Catherine's. It is in the Parish of Kileilagh. Between Spanish Point and this Taumple na Spannig, a great part of the Spanish Armada, was wrecked, and all that were on board these ships, that were flung by the tempest into the Parish of Kileilagh, were buried in this spot. There was an Oak Table on board one of these ships, probably the admirals, of curious workmanship; it was given by Boetius Clancy, who was the then inheritor of the place (also High Sheriff of the County), to Connor O'Brien, his brother-in-law. And it is still in high preservation in the Hall of Dromoland Castle. The House of St. Catherine's is now only occasionally used, but there is in it a private Theatre, in which within the last few years, Amateurs, the favoured guests of Mr. and Mrs. J. O'Brien, rivalled the old performances, which made the Kilkenny Theatricals so celebrated in the last century. To those who love the sea side, the fields behind Doolin House suffice for rest and quiet enjoyment; others may tempt the pools and their moving attractions, or the little sandy coves with their burdens of brilliant shells; of these may be named specimens of the Mollusca, Crustacea, Echinodermata, Actinozoa. The Ianthina are often wafted to these shores with their attendant semi-mollusks. It might be worth dredging here for the Ahera, a kind of shells found in Galway Bay, also the Pictunculus, and other unknown specialities on these untried shores. Indeed Cocoa Nuts and other tropical fruits and berries are often cast up by the prevailing West and South West winds which blow across the path way of the Gulph stream upon these shores.

The coast road by Mr. Johnston's of Aranview, and the cliffs, on a fine day in summer or autumn, give a charming variety of land and sea views, and the rocky pass on the return by Ballinalaken exhibits a savage wildness, which reminds one of the boldest conceptions of the great Murillo. The walk by the cliffs from the north is a treat; and the bathing in certain sandy nooks, when tide serves and wind is propitious, is very good indeed.

THE SEVENTH EXCURSION

may be just mentioned for the daring spirits who would venture into the fragile canvas canoe that rises like a sea bird on her native wave: this is to the

ISLES OF ARRAN

There are no islands on the shores of England, Ireland, or Scotland, of deeper interest than these. The wondrous fortresses of a mysterious race, driven to their last retreat, long before the Christian era, are here. No Cahirs on the main land can equal them. The Ethnological Section of the British Association visited them in 1857; only two expressions are now quoted on the subject. Mr. C. C. Barrington of Cambridge stated that "the ancient buildings in these islands, with all their singular interest, were scarcely known beyond the Channel. The peculiar grandeur of the antiquities of Aran was utterly unknown to him." Dr. Simpson of Edinburgh, as a Scotchman, added "that if the Scotch antiquarians are ever to study the antiquities of their country, it is through the medium of the antiquities of Ireland." And as to Ecclesiastical remains and that wondrous fountain of Missionary enterprize which filled Burren's wildest hills and most gloomy glens with Oratories and Churches some of them over 13 centuries ago, - a visit to Arran and the study of its history will give full satisfaction. In fact Iona was not to the barbarous adjacent main land of Scotland more a blessing than Arran to the Pagans of Burren and Corcomroe. The best of the churches was demolished to make a Cromwellian fortress; and Petty, in his "Anatomy," tells of wages to the artillerymen.

The steamer which runs from Galway on a fine day might take a party in two hours or less, and cruise homewards under the cliffs of Moher and disembark the passengers at Ballahaline.

ON PISCATORIAL EXCURSIONS

a word may be added. Goller, a little lake in the bog near Lisdoonvarna, may be fished off the shore, and the cunning Waltonian take home a nice basket of little trout. Lickeen Lake, near Kilfenora, is of some considerable size. The fish are not large, but are very plenty and hungry. On a fine Summer evening, when a little midge flits from the flowering meadowsweet and in countless numbers sits upon the waters, the "gosling greenfly" will prove most enticing. By day, in July and August, a curious coleopterous insect, with a very blue and lake-coloured body, frequents the rocks, and when he takes to the water is snapped at with avidity. Curious it is that none of the rivers running into the

Atlantic have any perch, pike or roach. At the flag on the Derry river one may take white trout as a flood is clearing off, but it is netted and poached too. The destruction caused to the valuable waters of the district is deplorable; anywhere else they would get fair play and pay well - indeed water well preserved is worth far more, acre for acre, than the richest bullock-fattening lands. But if we would take good brown trout or large pike, the latter may be fished for in Inchiquin Lake by day, and the former by night, or in Ballycullinan Lake - indeed O'Gorman mentions pike taken by him from 10 to 20 and 40 pounds; and an Inchiquin pike plays like a salmon. Those who know Inchiquin and other Clare waters have smiled at the exulatation with which the Hon. G. Berkeley has described his capture of a pike of 13 or 14 pounds weight in some English preserve, and at the way in which he spreads the account of the glorious feat over a whole page of his charming book.

And now that these excursions must terminate, and the analysis of the waters is fully known, and their virtues practically experienced, a word may be said before

OUR FAREWELL.

In 1681 was published a work now before us, "A Tract on British Baths, with observations, hydrostatic, chromatic, and miscellaneous, setting forth explicitly the nature, property and distribution of each of the wells at Bath." It was written by Dr. Thomas Guidotti, and bears the imprimatur of the

President of the Medical College, London. It contains a century of cures, and the parties cured give details in a kind of votive declaration. It contains also prayers by Bishop Kenne, with pious counsels and expressions of gratitude to the "Giver of Health."

But whilst Bath and other watering places have been thus written up and their virtues magnified, Lisdoonvarna has been neglected or else written of in such a way as to give the public but a very poor impression of the virtue of the waters, and of the healthy and interesting country around it. But Lisdoonvarna Spa is a reality as a powerful medical application when rightly used. Thousands have tried it with good effect, and thousands more will try it again and again, with equal benefit. To all those who have, or yet may, come, are offered the ten thousand welcomes of Irish hearts, and for such it is hoped that health and happiness may be the result of their visit, not unassociated with some kindly impressions of the efforts to guide them through the wild regions of the West.

New Church for Lisdoonvarna
COUNTY CLARE.

~~~~~~

The reputation of Lisdoonvarna having for many years increased, as a most desirable resort for the Invalid and Tourist, a church was built in the year 1859 adequate to the requirements of the numbers who at that time frequented the place; and thus the recipients of health and strength who resorted thither enjoyed the opportunity of raising the voice of prayer, and offering the sacrifice of prayer and thanksgiving.

The stream of visitors having now swelled far in excess of all former calculation, and the place being certain to become most fashionable and largely frequented as the unique character of the Spas becomes more widely known and the facility of access improved, it is necessary to erect another church to afford accommodation to at least two hundred worshippers, and capable of further extension - this necessity was painfully exemplified during the last two seasons, when numbers had to retire, being unable to obtain either sitting or standing room.

The cost of erecting such a structure in a convenient central position, of suitable dimensions and of that grave and becoming character which the Church of Ireland would provide for her sons and her friends, cannot be estimated at less than £3,000.

An earnest appeal is made to the Christian liberality of the members of the Church of Ireland, of her friends, and of the sojourners at Lisdoonvarna as the local resources are limited, and the proposed expenditure is undertaken for the benefit of those who have recourse to the unrivalled Spas of Lisdoonvarna.

Contributions will be received by Richard Nugent, Esq., 32, Charing Cross, London ; R. Giles, Esq., Manager Munster Bank, Ennistymon, County Clare ; Rev. J.R. Copley, Deanery House, Kilfenora, or by any member of the Committee, and duly acknowledged in Irish and English papers.

ATLANTIC VIEW HOTEL,

LISDOONVARNA,

AUSTIN O'BRIEN, Proprietor.

———◆———

THIS HOTEL

is situated but a short distance from the famous Sulphur Spring, on an elevation commanding a view of the

"ATLANTIC OCEAN."

Extensive accommodation has been added since last season -

LADIES' DRAWING ROOM, SITTING - ROOM, NEW COFFEE ROOM

AND

KITCHEN, STABLES, CARRIAGE HOUSES, &c.

The internal arrangement will be under the immediate superintendence of the *Proprietor and his lady*.

———

N.B.-Prompt Attention, Cleanliness, and Moderate Charges.

———

As you find us
Recommend us.

QUEEN'S HOTEL COMPANY
(LIMITED).
LISDOONVARNA.

The above HOTEL has been, for the Third Season, opened for the reception of visitors,

UNDER THE MANAGEMENT OF
JOHN R. ANNESLEY
(LATE PROPRIETOR),

who has experience as Messman for fourteen years, and late House Steward of some of the First Clubs in Ireland for ten years.

THE CUISINE DEPARTMENT
is under his immediate superintendence.

THE HOTEL,

which is second to none, stands on an elevation, having a view of the sea from the ground floor, and the beautiful coast scenery extending from Hag's Head to Black Head.

THE SULPHUR, IRON & MAGNESIA SPRINGS
are within 100 yards of the HOTEL, and
THE PUBLIC BATHS ARE NOW OPEN.

VISITORS FROM DUBLIN, &c.,

can make the journey in one day *via* Galway to Ballyvaughan and the far-famed Corkscrew Road.

Two well-appointed Long Cars leave Ennis daily for the convenience of the visitors coming by that route. Full information as to terms, &c., can be obtained by application to the Manager,

JOHN ROSS ANNESLEY.

THE EAGLE HOTEL

LISDOONVARNA.

WILLIAM BUTLER , Proprietor.

This Favourite Establishment, which has recently undergone extensive improvements, and is approached by a new and handsome road, is very near to the principal Wells, possesses everything requisite to promote the comfort and convenience of Visitors and Tourists to the famed

SPAS OF LISDOONVARNA.

It contains

FIFTY BEDROOMS, A VERY SPACIOUS COFFEE - ROOM,

A DRAWING - ROOM FOR LADIES AND FAMILIES,

OTHER HANDSOME SITTING - ROOMS,

SMOKING - ROOMS, BILLIARDS, &c.,

AND A BOAT

for the use of the Visitors stopping at the Hotel, on Lough Gollard.

Good Trout Fishing on the Lake.

THE POSTING IS COMPLETE IN ALL ITS BRANCHES.

Table d'Hote every Day.

THE ATLANTIC HOTEL,

MILTOWN MALBAY,

HENRY LIGHTLY , Proprietor.

———— ❖ ————

THE proprietor begs to inform his friends and the public that he is now, for the second year, conducting the above Hotel, which has recently undergone considerable improvements calculated to promote the comfort of casual visitors and of families sojourning. The House is one of the most beautifully situated and spacious Hotels in the United Kingdom, comprising Reception, Ball, and coffee-rooms, together with several suites of private apartments, and airy bedrooms abundant, not to mention bath-rooms and accommodation for visitors' servants and for carriages and horses.

The House may be said to hang over the Atlantic Ocean, the sprays often striking the windows in a storm.

The scenery is most beautiful on the Western Coast, just midway between the Cliffs of Moher, on the North, and those of Kilkee, on the South.

Lisdoonvarna and Ennis are fifteen miles distant from the Hotel. The celebrated Ogham Inscriptia, Mount Callan, is only four miles from the Hotel. The immediate neighbourhood is highly respectable. There is excellent sea, river, and lake fishing available. The sea-bathing and the salubrity of the air cannot be exceeded for health-giving qualities. There is a daily post, and telegraphic communication convenient, also a Place of Worship in Miltownmalbay town.

The proprietor will spare no expense or trouble to provide the best viands and liquors, and to promote the comfort of those visiting this First-class Hotel.

Full information as to terms, &c., can be obtained by application to the proprietor.

May 25th, 1876.

Midland Great Western Railway.

---◆---

SUMMER EXCURSIONS
TO THE
WEST OF IRELAND

---◆---

MONTHLY TOURIST TICKETS
Are issued from BROADSTONE TERMINUS, Dublin,
TO ENNIS,
Via ATHENRY, returning from KILRUSH, *via* Limerick
and Athenry,
Available for the LISDOONVARNA and KILKEE TOUR;
Also
To BALLYVAUGHAN and BACK, *via* Galway,
In connection with the Steamer *"Citie of the Tribes,"*
Being the **Cheapest, Shortest** and **Most Enjoyable** Route
TO THE
CELEBRATED SPAS OF LISDOONVARNA.

From Dublin to Galway in *Five and a Half Hours;* from Galway
to Ballyvaughan, by the Steamer, in *One Hour;* and thence to
Lisdoonvarna by well appointed Omnibus or Cars in *One
Hour.*

* * A considerable reduction is made in the price of Tickets for
parties of *Two* to *Six* Passengers. The time can be extended on a
payment of a small per centage.

An Illustrated Prospectus of all the Circular tours in connection with
the Midland Great Western system, containing Skeleton Routes for
Tours of a week or fortnight, "DESCRIPTIVE GUIDE" to the places named,
and "ANGLER'S COMPANION," with Map of the Fishing Districts, may be
obtained, with every further information required, on application to
the MANAGER'S OFFICE, BROADSTONE TERMINUS, DUBLIN. *Price (postage
included)* 3d.

J. E. WARD, MANAGER

BROADSTONE, DUBLIN, *June 1876.*

Great Southern & Western Railway.

CIRCULAR TOURS.

From 1st JUNE to 31st OCTOBER, 1876,
MONTHLY TOURIST TICKETS
Can be obtained at KINGSBRIDGE STATION, Dublin, to
enable holders to visit
KILLARNEY, LIMERICK, CONNEMARA, GALWAY,
And other places of interest in the SOUTH and WEST,
at the following Fares, subject to the Conditions which
are shown in the Company's Time Tables and on the
Coupons :

FARES FROM DUBLIN :-

			1st. Class.			2nd Class.		
			£	s.	d.	£	s.	d.
Ticket for One Passenger		...	3	1	6	2	2	0
"	Two Passengers	...	5	10	6	3	15	6
"	Three "	...	7	16	6	5	7	6
"	Four "	...	9	16	0	6	13	6
"	Five "	...	11	10	0	7	16	6
"	Six "	...	12	17	6	8	16	0

Available on any day within One Calendar Month after date of issue.

Holders of above tickets return to Dublin (BROADSTONE) by the
Midland Great Western Railway.

Fares do not include conveyance by road, but the Railway
fares between Killarney and Galway and between Westport
and Ballina are included.

Passengers may break journey at Limerick Junction or
Mallow, and those desirous of visiting Cork can do so by
paying the fare between Mallow and Cork.

By Order

Kingsbridge Terminus, Dublin, May, 1876.